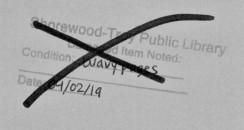

# Buddha Bowls

# Buddha Bowls

## 100 Nourishing One-Bowl Meals

### Kelli Foster

HARVARD COMMON PRESS

Inspiring | Educating | Creating | Entertaining

Brimming with creative inspiration, how-to projects, and useful information to enrich your everyday life, Quarto Knows is a favorite destination for those pursuing their interests and passions. Visit our site and dig deeper with our books into your area of interest: Quarto Creates, Quarto Cooks, Quarto Homes, Quarto Lives, Quarto Drives, Quarto Explores, Quarto Gifts, or Quarto Kids.

First Published in 2018 by The Harvard Common Press, an imprint of The Quarto Group, 100 Cummings Center, Suite 265-D, Beverly, MA 01915, USA.
T (978) 282-9590 F (978) 283-2742 QuartoKnows.com

The Harvard Common Press titles are also available at discount for retail, wholesale, promotional, and bulk purchase. For details, contact the Special Sales Manager by email at specialsales@quarto.com or by mail at The Quarto Group, Attn: Special Sales Manager, 401 Second Avenue North, Suite 310, Minneapolis, MN 55401, USA.

22 21 20 19 18          1 2 3 4 5

ISBN: 978-1-55832-915-7

Digital edition published in 2018
eISBN: 978-1-55832-916-4

Library of Congress Cataloging-in-Publication Data available.

Design & Page Layout: Allison Meierding
Photography: Maria Siriano

Printed in China

One of the things I love most about
food is its ability to bring people together.
Not just at the table but across time.

To Kate: Your spirit is a constant inspiration.

# Contents

Beautiful Buddha Bowls:
A Cook's Introduction      8

Basic Sauces and Dressings
for Buddha Bowls      15

Breakfast Bowls      29

Fish and Seafood Bowls      55

Chicken and Turkey Bowls      77

Beef and Lamb Bowls      97

Vegetable Bowls      115

Fruit Bowls      157

Acknowledgments      170

About the Author      170

Index      171

# Beautiful Buddha Bowls:
## A COOK'S INTRODUCTION

### WHAT ARE BUDDHA BOWLS?

First things first—what exactly are Buddha bowls? To me, they are one of the easiest ways to eat healthy and nourish my body with a wholesome, balanced meal any time of day.

You might know them as power bowls, bliss bowls, nourish bowls, or hippie bowls, but no matter what name they go by, Buddha bowls are a wholesome one-bowl meal packed with an assortment of nourishing, real-food ingredients. It's the kind of meal you feel really good about eating.

Buddha bowls are a well-balanced mix of protein, vegetables, and good fats that nourish you with a hearty, satisfying meal. Each bowl starts with a base typically made up of whole grains, rice, noodles, or legumes, or even a combination of those ingredients. Then it gets loaded with a generous assortment of cooked or raw vegetables, often a handful or two of fresh greens, and a boost of protein, from meat, fish, eggs, tofu, or beans, before getting finished off with a dressing, sauce, or broth. It all comes together in a big bowl, for an easy, healthy meal.

In the pages of this book, you'll find a versatile mix of easy, healthy Buddha bowl recipes for breakfast, lunch, dinner, and even dessert. Each Buddha bowl has a little bit of the familiar mixed with fresh—and sometimes unexpected—ingredients to keep every bowl feeling new and exciting, and always deeply nourishing. My hope is that these recipes delight and inspire you to create your own unique bowls.

There are a lot of theories about how these stuffed bowls got their name, though there really isn't one that's universally agreed upon. One of the most common explanations is that these overstuffed bowls are named for the likeness to the rounded belly of the Buddha.

### BUILDING A BUDDHA BOWL

Building a Buddha bowl is like one of those choose-your-own-adventure books. There are no strict rules and creativity is highly encouraged. In fact, Buddha bowls require more of a template and some inspiration rather than recipes that are set in stone. It's a meal that's incredibly versatile and highly adaptable, which means swapping different ingredients in or out of any recipe is always easy. Get the foundation for building a Buddha bowl down and you'll see endless possibilities for how easy it is to make them your own.

When building Buddha bowls, I like to break the meal down into four basic components: grains, a protein, vegetables and fruit, and sauce, plus an extra finishing touch.

Let's take a look at each one.

## Grains, Noodles, and Beyond

Quinoa and brown rice are two of the most common bowl food bases, but they only scratch the surface of the realm of possibilities. Whole grains—including barley, buckwheat, freekeh, millet, and wild rice, just to name a few—are all fair game. These are high-fiber foods that provide carbohydrates, and in some cases a punch of protein.

But grains are just one option! Remember, versatility reigns supreme, so noodles like soba or rice noodles, even vegetable noodles and alternative "grains," like riced cauliflower or broccoli, are also great choices for your bowl base.

In the next section you'll find a helpful guide for cooking each type of bowl base, and a few tricks for making even more flavorful grains, rice, and noodles.

## Protein

A wholesome source of protein is what gives this one-bowl meal substance and plays an important roll in filling you up. Regardless of whether you're cooking up a Buddha bowl for breakfast, lunch, or dinner, protein is a must. Some bowls will include meat, chicken, fish, or eggs while vegetarian and vegan bowls rely on tofu, tempeh, beans, and legumes as the main protein source. Even nuts, seeds, certain grains, or a spoonful of Greek yogurt can make a bowl more filling.

## Vegetables and Fruit

Vegetables are the heart and soul of any Buddha bowl, and make up about half of the bowl. This is where anything goes: All types of produce—cooked, raw, or a mix of the two—are fair game. A variety of vegetables not only makes for a more colorful meal, but it also means a variety of tastes and textures that instantly creates a more interesting bowl.

## Dressing, Sauce, or Broth

No Buddha bowl is complete without something saucy to top it off! This is the final element that takes a Buddha bowl from good to great. It doesn't matter if it's a creamy sauce or pesto, a tangy dressing, or a savory broth—any one will do. It's the finishing touch that adds another dimension of flavor and ties all the ingredients together. When made with healthy oils, nut butter, yogurt, or avocado, sauces and dressings are a source of good fats, which also aid in making your bowl more filling.

I know I mentioned that Buddha bowls have just four components, and they do—*but* a little something extra in the way of a topping or garnish is always a good idea. Finishing off your Buddha bowl with some toasted nuts or seeds, kimchi or sauerkraut, or fresh herbs is optional but highly recommended. Not only does it make any bowl look great, but it also adds texture, crunch, a tangy twist, or a pop of freshness that makes your bowl feel more special.

Each recipe includes suggested toppings and garnishes that complement the bowl, though you'll notice that unlike the other ingredients in the recipe, the amount is not specified. Use a little or use a lot—this part is entirely up to you.

## EMBRACE THE MEANWHILE

"Embrace the meanwhile" is one of my favorite mantras in the kitchen, and it's particularly useful when making Buddha bowls. It is a smart and helpful tactic that helps you maximize your time in the kitchen, work more efficiently, and get your bowls on the table faster. Sounds good, right?

It takes advantage of those hands-off minutes that so often show up in recipes—like when a pot of grains are cooking or vegetables are roasting—and allows you to work on something else, like whisking together the sauce or dressing for your bowl.

Instead of prepping all the ingredients for a recipe at the outset, prep just what you need to start, then work as you go. This will look different from recipe to recipe, though the idea remains the same.

## THE BEST BOWL FOR THE JOB

Just as important as the wholesome ingredients you pile into your Buddha bowl is the bowl you serve them in. The very first step in making any Buddha bowl is choosing the best bowl for the job. Some bowls are better than others for this type of meal.

So, what is the best bowl for the job? Rule number one when reaching for a bowl to build your meal: Bigger is always better. Remember, this is a meal that piles the grains, protein, and veggies into a single bowl. I always choose a bowl that's big enough to fit all the components so that my food is not spilling over the sides, but not so big that my food gets lost.

There's also the bowl shape to consider: Do you go with wide and shallow, or deep and narrow? Large, wide, shallow bowls are my go-to for non-brothy Buddha bowls, most dinner bowls, and any recipes that include bigger ingredients, like a salmon fillet, wide-cut wedges of tofu, sprawling fried eggs, or big piles of veggies. Deeper, narrow bowls are a great choice of most breakfast bowls, brothy bowls, and sweet dessert bowls.

# Grain Guide

## YOUR GUIDE TO COOKING ANY GRAIN

I don't know about you, but no matter how many times I cook rice and grains (which is often!) I never seem to remember the right ratio of grains to water, or how long they each take to cook. That's why we all need a cheat sheet to help us remember. The one on page 13 is yours!

Even though each recipe walks you through how to cook the grain or rice that's called for, I think it's so helpful to have it all laid out in one convenient location. Use the chart as a reference any time you're cooking a pot of grains—for any of the recipes in this book and beyond.

Making a bowl that calls for quinoa, but you'd rather use farro? Go right ahead! The chart will help you figure out the right amount of liquid and the proper cook time.

There's another stovetop method for cooking rice and grains that skips the measuring altogether—the pasta method. As the name implies, this approach is really not much different than cooking a pot of pasta. Cover the rice or grains with an ample amount of water (about 2 inches [5 cm] is a good rule of thumb), then cook until the grains are tender and drain off the excess water. This method is particularly useful when cooking big batches of rice and grains.

## GIVE GRAINS MORE FLAVOR

Want to infuse even more flavor into a pot of grains? It's really easy and doesn't take much time or effort. Although water is the cooking liquid we use most often, it's far from the only option. For an easy swap, use stock or broth in place of some or all of the water for a more savory, full-flavored taste.

Tea, fruit juice, and vegetable juice are other great options for giving a pot of grains a more intriguing flavor. Juices, like orange, carrot, and beet, can also really up the flavor and even impart a pretty hue. If you decide to cook grains with tea or juice, the best results come from cooking with a blend of water and tea or juice. These liquids can have a strong flavor, and a little goes a long way. Use too much and food can easily be overpowered, taking on an overly sweet or bitter taste. As a rule of thumb, stir in no more than 50 percent tea or juice.

But getting creative with cooking liquids is just one way to add more flavor to a pot of grains. You can also infuse more flavor with vegetable trimmings, herb stems and leaves, smashed garlic cloves, hard cheese rinds, and whole spices. Add any one or a combination of these ingredients to the pot at the beginning of cooking and the flavor will be subtly infused into your rice or grains.

One of my all-time favorite ways to up the flavor of a pot of grains is by toasting the grains or rice before cooking. Start by heating a pat of butter or small glug of oil in a saucepan, then stir in the grains or rice, so they're well coated. Cook over medium-low heat for a few minutes, and they pick up a wonderful warm and nutty, toasted aroma that will carry through to the finished bowl. They might even pick up a little more color as well. Once the grains are toasted just the way you like them, add liquid, and cook as usual.

## ACE ALTERNATIVE "GRAINS"

In addition to traditional grains and noodles, I've included several Buddha bowl recipes that use gluten-free grain alternatives, like riced cauliflower and broccoli, as well as zucchini, sweet potato, and beet noodles. Now, you're certainly not going to confuse vegetable rices and noodles for the real thing, but that's not the point. I like this alternative because sometimes I just want an extra serving of vegetables in my bowl, because I'd prefer to keep my meal gluten free, or even because sometimes I have produce that needs to get used up.

Vegetable rices and noodles are hitting the shelves of more and more grocery stores every day. But it's also easy (and usually less expensive) to make many of them at home. Here's how:

**Cauliflower Rice:** Cauliflower rice is made from both the stem and the florets of the vegetable. Remove and discard the bottom portion of the stem. Cut the head into small pieces and add to the bowl of a food processor fitted with the blade attachment. Pulse several times, at 1- to 2-second bursts, until the pieces are broken down into rice-like grains. One medium head of cauliflower yields about 16 ounces (455 g) of rice.

**Broccoli Rice:** Broccoli rice is made from the firm stems of the vegetable. Start by cutting the thick stem away from the head of florets. Trim any side shoots or leaves and peel away the fibrous, woody outer layer of the stem with a vegetable peeler. Cut the stem into 2-inch (5 cm) pieces and add to the bowl of a food processor fitted with the blade attachment. Pulse several times, at 1- to 2-second bursts, until the pieces are broken down into rice-like grains. Two large stems yield approximately 8 ounces (225 g) of broccoli rice.

| 1 Cup Dried Grains | Cooking Liquid | Cook Time | Stovetop Method | Yield |
|---|---|---|---|---|
| Amaranth | 2 to 3 cups (470 to 705 ml) | 20 to 25 minutes | Combine with liquid in a saucepan; bring to a boil; lower heat, then cover and simmer | 2½ cups (415 g) |
| Barley (pearled) | 3 cups (705 ml) | 30 to 45 minutes | | 3 cups (495 g) |
| Buckwheat (kasha) | 2 cups (470 ml) | 20 minutes | | 4 cups (660 g) |
| Bulgur | 2 cups (470 ml) | 10 to 15 minutes | | 3 cups (495 g) |
| Farro (pearled) | 2½ cups (590 ml) | 30 to 40 minutes | | 3 cups (495 g) |
| Freekeh (cracked) | 2½ cups (590 ml) | 20 minutes | | Just over 2 cups (330 g) |
| Millet | 2 to 2½ cups (470 to 590 ml) | 20 to 25 minutes | | 4 cups (600 g) |
| Noodles, Rice | - | 5 to 10 minutes | Soak in boiling water, according to package instructions | - |
| Noodles, Soba | - | 10 minutes | Pasta method (see page 11) | - |
| Quinoa | 2 cups (470 ml) | 15 to 20 minutes | Combine with liquid in a saucepan; bring to a boil; lower heat and simmer; steam with lid on for 5 minutes | 3 cups (555 g) |
| Rice, Brown | 2 cups (470 ml) | 40 to 45 minutes | Combine with liquid in a saucepan; bring to a boil; lower heat, then cover and simmer; steam with lid on for 10 minutes | 3 cups (495 g) |
| Rice, Forbidden (Black) | 2 cups (470 ml) | 30 to 40 minutes | Combine with liquid in a saucepan; bring to a boil; lower heat, then cover and simmer | 3 cups (495 g) |
| Rice, Jasmine | 1½ cups (355 ml) | 25 minutes | Combine with liquid in a saucepan; bring to a boil; lower heat, then cover and simmer; steam with lid on for 10 minutes | 3 cups (495 g) |
| Rice, Wild | - | 50 minutes | Pasta method (see page 11) | 3½ cups (495 g) |
| Steel-Cut Oats | 4 cups (940 ml) | 30 minutes | Bring liquid to a boil; add oats; return to a boil; lower heat and simmer uncovered | 3 cups (495 g) |

# Basic Sauces and **Dressings** for BUDDHA BOWLS

Avocado Green Goddess Dressing **16**

Avocado Sauce **17**

Basic Everyday Vinaigrette **18**

Chimichurri Sauce **19**

Creamy Feta Sauce **20**

Essential Pesto Sauce with Any Herb or Leafy Greens **21**

Light and Creamy Goat Cheese Sauce **22**

Miso-Ginger Sauce **23**

Peanut Sauce **24**

Raita **25**

Roasted Red Pepper Sauce **25**

Tahini Sauce **26**

Yogurt Sauce **27**

# Avocado Green Goddess Dressing

Green Goddess dressing is a cool and creamy, herb and garlic sauce conceived in San Francisco in the 1920s, with a popular resurgence in the '70s and '80s. Here, it gets a healthy, fresh spin by putting lush avocado and Greek yogurt at the forefront for an incredibly creamy dressing, packed with good fats to help make any bowl more satisfying and filling.

**Makes about ¾ cup (180 ml)**

1 medium ripe avocado
¼ cup (60 g) plain Greek yogurt
3 tablespoons (9 g) packed snipped chives
3 tablespoons (9 g) packed fresh basil
3 tablespoons (9 g) packed fresh parsley
1 clove garlic
2 tablespoons (30 ml) avocado oil or extra-virgin olive oil
2 tablespoons (30 ml) apple cider vinegar
2 tablespoons (30 ml) freshly squeezed lemon juice
½ teaspoon kosher salt
¼ teaspoon freshly ground black pepper
5 tablespoons (75 ml) water

Combine the avocado, yogurt, herbs, garlic, oil, vinegar, lemon juice, salt, and pepper in the bowl of a food processor. Blend continuously until smooth and well combined, scraping down the sides of the bowl as necessary. With the food processor running, add the water, 1 tablespoon (15 ml) at a time, until it reaches the desired consistency.

**Try It Here!**
· Summertime Green Goddess Steak Bowls, page 99
· Green Goddess Quinoa Bowls with Crispy Tofu, page 119
· Beet Falafel Bowls, page 150

**Note:** The sauce can be stored in an airtight container in the refrigerator for up to 3 days.

# Avocado Sauce

Calling all avocado lovers! If avocado is a regular addition to your Buddha bowls, here's how to turn your favorite produce into a rich and creamy, pourable sauce that goes with everything. This sauce is a great way to use up overripe avocados that are on their last leg, though firm avocados will benefit from an extra couple of days to soften.

The avocado is blended and thinned with water and fresh citrus juice in a food processor for a sauce that comes together in minutes. Give it some extra flair with a spoonful of tangy Greek yogurt or a handful of herbs.

Place the ingredients in the bowl of a food processor of blender. Process continuously until well combined and smooth, about 1 minute.

**VARIATIONS:**
- **Avocado-Yogurt Sauce:** Add 2 tablespoons (30 g) Greek yogurt
- **Herbed Avocado Sauce:** Add ¼ cup (12 g) loosely packed fresh herbs (cilantro, basil, mint, dill)

**Makes about 1 cup (235 ml)**

1 ripe avocado, peeled and pitted
½ cup (120 ml) water
Juice from 1 lemon or lime
1 clove garlic
¼ teaspoon kosher salt
¼ teaspoon freshly ground black pepper

**Try It Here!**
- Black Bean and Chorizo Bowls, page 46
- Balsamic Shrimp and Farro Bowls, page 72
- Steak Fajita Spaghetti Squash Bowls, page 98
- Chili-Lime Portobello Bowls, page 154

**Note:** The sauce can be stored in an airtight container in the refrigerator for up to 3 days.

# Basic Everyday Vinaigrette

Every home cook should have a basic vinaigrette recipe in their arsenal, for Buddha bowls and beyond. This is the much-loved, tried-and-true version I've been making for years. To get the most out of it, I encourage you to approach it as a flexible template rather than a set recipe. Experiment with different vinegars, lemon, or other types of citrus juice to vary the flavor profile of your vinaigrette.

**Makes about ¾ cup (180 ml)**

⅓ cup (80 ml) freshly squeezed lemon juice or vinegar, such as balsamic, apple cider, white wine, red wine, or rice vinegar
1 tablespoon (11 g) Dijon mustard
1 clove garlic, minced
⅓ cup (80 ml) extra-virgin olive oil
½ teaspoon kosher salt
¼ teaspoon freshly ground black pepper

**Note:** The dressing can be stored in an airtight container in the refrigerator for up to 5 days.

Combine all the ingredients in a small jar. Shake well until the dressing is emulsified. Use immediately or store in the refrigerator until ready to serve.

**VARIATIONS:**
- **Lemon-Herb Vinaigrette:** Add 2 tablespoons (30 ml) white balsamic vinegar and 2 tablespoons (6 g) finely chopped herbs
- **White Wine–Lemon Vinaigrette:** Use ¼ cup (60 ml) freshly squeezed lemon juice and 2 tablespoons (30 ml) white wine vinegar

**Try It Here!**
- Lentil and Smoked Salmon Niçoise Bowls, page 56

# Chimichurri Sauce

Chimichurri, the vibrant green sauce that hails from Argentina, is an herb lover's dream come true. With nearly a bundle of herbs plus a splash of lemon and vinegar, it is bright and bold, with a fresh tang that livens up everything it touches, from fish and vegetables to chicken and meat.

Add the herbs, garlic, and salt to the bowl of a food processor. Pulse in 2-second bursts until the herbs are finely chopped. Scrape down the sides of the bowl. With the motor running, slowly pour in the oil, lemon juice, and vinegar, and process until well combined, about 1 minute.

**Try It Here!**
- Brown Rice Bowls with Seared Fish and Chimichurri, page 75
- Chimichurri Chicken Bowls, page 87
- Lamb and Roasted Cauliflower Taco Bowls with Chimichurri, page 113
- Chipotle Sweet Potato Bowls, page 145

**Makes about ¾ cup (180 ml)**

1 packed cup (16 g) cilantro leaves
½ packed cup (24 g) parsley leaves
1 clove garlic
½ teaspoon kosher salt
⅓ cup (80 ml) extra-virgin olive oil
2 tablespoons (30 ml) freshly
    squeezed lemon juice
1 tablespoon (15 ml) red wine vinegar

**Note:** The sauce can be stored in an airtight container in the refrigerator for up to 4 days.

# Creamy Feta Sauce

If you have a thing for briny feta cheese, you are going to love this sauce. It's blended together with a few basic kitchen staples for a super easy, creamy sauce to be drizzled over everything from vegetable bowls to ones topped with chicken, meat, and fish. Give it a simple twist with a handful of your favorite herbs or a roasted red pepper for a pop of color and hint of smokiness.

**Makes about ½ cup (120 ml)**

4 ounces (115 g) crumbled feta,
    at room temperature
3 tablespoons (45 ml) water
1 tablespoon (15 ml) extra-virgin
    olive oil
½ teaspoon kosher salt

**Note:** The sauce can be stored in an airtight container in the refrigerator for up to 4 days.

1 Place all the ingredients in the bowl of a food processor or blender. Process continuously until the sauce is smooth, 1 to 2 minutes. Thin with additional water, as desired.

2 Serve immediately or store in a covered container in the refrigerator until ready to use.

**VARIATIONS:**
- **Herbed Feta Sauce:** Add ¼ cup (12 g) finely chopped fresh herbs (basil, cilantro, dill, mint, parsley, tarragon)
- **Roasted Red Pepper and Feta Sauce:** Add 1 roasted red pepper

**Try It Here!**
- Harissa Chicken Bowls, page 83
- Greek Power Bowls, page 107
- Stuffed Eggplant Bowls with Spiced Lamb, page 108

# Essential Pesto Sauce with Any Herb or Leafy Greens

If I could have only one type of sauce on my Buddha bowls, it would be this pesto, no question about it! It's fresh, and so unbelievably versatile, and a small spoonful of miso paste adds the most irresistible savory depth. We most often associate basil with pesto sauce, but in fact, it can be made with any type of greens or fresh herbs, or even a combination of the two. Use this recipe as your template, and substitute in your greens of choice, along with any type of nuts or seeds.

Add the herbs or greens, nuts, cheese, lemon juice, miso paste, and garlic to the bowl of a food processor or blender. Pulse until finely chopped. Gradually pour in the olive oil while processing continuously.

**Try It Here!**
- Spinach and Mushroom Pesto Breakfast Bowls, page 44
- Winter Squash and Farro Macro Bowls, page 149
- Crispy White Bean and Pesto Bowls, page 117

**Makes ½ cup (120 ml)**

2 cups (96 g) loosely packed herbs
    or leafy greens
2 tablespoons (18 g) toasted nuts
    or seeds
2 tablespoons (10 g) grated Parmesan
    or Pecorino cheese
1 tablespoon (15 ml) freshly squeezed
    lemon juice
1 teaspoon (5 g) miso paste
1 clove garlic
¼ cup (60 ml) extra-virgin olive oil

**Note:** The sauce can be stored in an airtight container in the refrigerator for up to 5 days.

# Light and Creamy Goat Cheese Sauce

When I'm feeling a little indulgent, I get out my food processor and nubby log of soft goat cheese from the fridge, and in a matter of minutes I have a tangy and creamy sauce to drizzle over my Buddha bowls. I believe in buying good-quality ingredients, especially when they are the shining stars in a recipe, as the cheese is here.

**Makes about ½ cup (120 ml)**

4 ounces (115 g) goat cheese, at room temperature
1 tablespoon (15 ml) extra-virgin olive oil
2 tablespoons (30 ml) water
½ teaspoon kosher salt

Place all the ingredients in the bowl of a food processor or blender. Process continuously until the sauce is smooth, 1 to 2 minutes.

**VARIATION:**
• **Herbed Goat Cheese Sauce:** Add ¼ cup (12 g) chopped fresh herbs (basil, dill, mint, chives, tarragon)

**Note:** The sauce can be stored in an airtight container in the refrigerator for up to 4 days.

**Try It Here!**
• Peachy Basil Chicken and Rice Bowls, page 88
• Smoky Lemon Brussels Sprout Bowls with Turkey Meatballs, page 94
• Spring Soba Bowls, page 133

# Miso-Ginger Sauce

I didn't get acquainted with miso paste until well into my adult life, but it has become one of my favorite and most-used condiments, particularly white miso. It's an ultra-savory, umami-rich ingredient made primarily from fermented soybeans, and even just a small spoonful can bring a dish to life. Here, it's blended with cashews and a generous amount of fresh ginger for a full-flavored, creamy sauce.

1 Place all the ingredients in the bowl of a food processor or blender. Process continuously until the sauce is smooth, 2 to 3 minutes. Thin with additional water, as desired.

2 Serve immediately or store in a covered container in the refrigerator until ready to use.

**Try It Here!**
- Buckwheat and Black Bean Breakfast Bowls, page 48
- Salmon Teriyaki Bowls with Miso-Braised Kale, page 64
- Beef and Broccoli Bowls, page 100
- Korean-Style Beef Bowls with Zucchini Noodles, page 102
- Vegetarian Sushi Bowls, page 132

**Makes about ¾ cup (180 ml)**

¼ cup (36 g) raw unsalted cashews, soaked in water overnight and drained
¼ cup (60 ml) rice vinegar
2 tablespoons (30 g) white miso paste
2 tablespoons (30 ml) water
1 tablespoon (6 g) chopped fresh ginger
1½ teaspoons (7.5 ml) toasted sesame oil
1 teaspoon (6 g) honey
1 clove garlic, chopped
Freshly ground black pepper

**Note:** The sauce can be stored in an airtight container in the refrigerator for up to 4 days.

# Peanut Sauce

I've made many versions of peanut sauce over the years, and this one is my favorite because it really gives you the most bang for your buck. With just a handful of basic ingredients, it's quick and easy to pull together at a moment's notice, with pops of earthy, savory, and tangy flavors that make it anything but dull. There's also the option to jazz up basic peanut sauce with a few spoonfuls of Sriracha for a spicy punch, red curry paste for a hint of warm, aromatic heat, or some tamarind paste and a splash of fish sauce for sweet and savory undertones.

**Makes about 1 cup (235 ml)**

½ cup (130 g) creamy peanut butter
3 tablespoons (45 ml) soy sauce
2 tablespoons (30 ml) rice vinegar
3 tablespoons (45 ml) water
2 teaspoons (10 ml) toasted sesame oil
1 tablespoon (6 g) finely grated fresh ginger
¼ teaspoon cayenne pepper (optional)

**Note:** The sauce can be stored in an airtight container in the refrigerator for up to 4 days.

1 Combine all the ingredients in the bowl of a food processor or blender. Process continuously until smooth and well combined, about 2 minutes.

2 Serve immediately or store in a covered container in the refrigerator until ready to use.

**VARIATIONS:**
- **Curried Peanut Sauce:** Add 1 teaspoon (5 g) red curry paste
- **Spicy Peanut Sauce:** Add 1 to 2 tablespoons (15 to 30 ml) Sriracha
- **Tamarind Peanut Sauce:** Add 2 tablespoons (30 g) tamarind paste and 2 tablespoons (30 ml) fish sauce

**Try It Here!**
- Shrimp Summer Roll Bowls, page 69
- Spicy Thai Chicken and Brown Rice Bowls, page 89
- Ginger Beef Bowls, page 105
- Cauliflower Pad Thai Bowls, page 135
- Spicy Sesame Tofu and Rice Bowls, page 136
- Chili-Maple Tofu Bowls, page 139

# Raita

Raita is a cool, creamy Indian yogurt sauce, and this version is stirred together with cucumber, fresh herbs, and warm spices, like coriander and garam masala. It's a thick sauce you'll enjoy for taming spicy Buddha bowl ingredients, complementing roasted vegetables, and topping over rich pieces of fish.

Add the yogurt, cucumber, cilantro (or mint), lemon juice, spices, and salt to a small bowl. Mix together until well combined.

**Note:** The sauce can be stored in an airtight container in the refrigerator for up to 3 days.

**Try It Here!**
- Lamb Kebab Bowls, page 109
- Turmeric-Ginger Cauliflower and Lentil Bowls, page 143

**Makes about 1 cup (235 ml)**

1 cup (240 g) plain yogurt
¾ cup (90 g) shredded cucumber
2 tablespoons finely chopped cilantro (2 g) or mint (6 g)
1 teaspoon (5 ml) freshly squeezed lemon juice
½ teaspoon ground coriander
½ teaspoon ground garam masala
¼ teaspoon kosher salt

# Roasted Red Pepper Sauce

I always have a jar of roasted red peppers tucked away in the back of my pantry. I often buy a jar with grand plans to use them in a new recipe, but instead whirl them into this subtly textured, smoky sauce. I cannot stop making it! It's creamy and rich, almost decadent, yet totally healthy and surprisingly easy to pull together in just minutes.

Add all of the ingredients to the bowl of a food processor or blender. Process continuously until well blended and mostly smooth, 2 to 3 minutes.

**Note:** The sauce can be stored in an airtight container in the refrigerator for up to 5 days.

**Try It Here!**
- Almond-Quinoa and Salmon Bowls, page 87
- Herbed Chickpea and Bulgur Bowls, page 125
- Spiced Bean and Mushroom Bowls with Roasted Red Pepper Sauce, page 141

**Makes just over 1 cup (235 ml)**

1 (12-ounce, or 340 g) jar roasted red peppers, drained
¼ cup (36 g) unsalted toasted almonds
1 clove garlic
¼ cup (60 ml) extra-virgin olive oil
Juice from ½ lemon
1 teaspoon (2 g) paprika
Kosher salt and freshly ground pepper

# Tahini Sauce

This is the sauce I make more than any other for drizzling over Buddha bowls. It's wildly versatile and has a rich, earthy, and nutty taste that has a knack for pairing well with everything. And while I love basic creamy tahini sauce, I encourage you to get creative and change it up with the suggested variations below.

**Makes about ¾ cup (180 ml)**

⅓ cup (80 g) tahini
⅓ cup (80 ml) water
2 tablespoons (30 ml) freshly squeezed lemon juice
1 clove garlic, minced
½ teaspoon kosher salt
¼ teaspoon freshly ground black pepper

**Note:** The sauce can be stored in an airtight container in the refrigerator for up to 5 days.

Place all the ingredients in the bowl of a food processor or blender. Process continuously until well combined, 1 to 2 minutes. Thin with additional water, if desired.

**VARIATIONS:**
- **Dill Tahini Sauce:** Add ¼ cup (12 g) finely chopped fresh dill
- **Green Tahini Sauce:** Add ¼ cup (12 g) fresh parsley leaves, 2 tablespoons (2 g) fresh cilantro leaves, and 2 tablespoons (6 g) fresh dill
- **Lemon Tahini Sauce:** Use ¼ cup (60 ml) freshly squeezed lemon juice and 2 tablespoons (30 ml) water
- **Spicy Maple Tahini Sauce:** Swap freshly squeezed lemon juice for white wine vinegar, and add 1 tablespoon (15 ml) maple syrup and ¼ teaspoon cayenne pepper
- **Miso Tahini Sauce:** Add 2 teaspoons (10 g) miso paste
- **Spicy Tahini Sauce:** Add 1 teaspoon (2 g) harissa
- **Tangy Tahini Sauce:** Swap lemon juice for an equal amount of apple cider vinegar

**Try It Here!**
- Scrambled Chickpea Breakfast Bowls, page 49
- Tofu Scramble Bowls with Kale and Brussels Sprouts, page 52
- Superfood Salmon Bowls, page 74
- Freekeh Bowls with Caramelized Onions, Warm Tomatoes, and Seared Fish, page 73
- Warm Autumn Chicken and Wild Rice Bowls, page 85
- Dukkah-Crusted Chicken and Barley Bowls, page 82
- Herbed Chicken and Root Vegetable Bowls, page 93
- Miso Noodle Bowls with Stir-Fried Beef, page 103
- Lamb Meatball Bowls with Sweet Potato Noodles and Green Tahini, page 110
- Cauliflower Tabbouleh Bowls with Lamb Meatballs, page 112
- Super Green Quinoa Bowls, page 116
- Butternut Squash and Kale Bowls, page 126
- Broccoli Rice and Egg Bowls, page 134
- Harvest Macro Bowl, page 142

# Yogurt Sauce

This creamy yogurt sauce is a healthy finishing touch for any Buddha bowl, yet it always feels like something of a treat to me, most notably when it's doctored up with lemon juice and herbs for a play on ranch dressing. I prefer Greek yogurt for this sauce for its thick texture and tangy flavor, and of course, the extra boost of protein, though it's worth noting that any type of plain yogurt will work just fine.

Place the ingredients in a medium mixing bowl, and whisk until well combined.

**VARIATIONS:**
- **Herb Yogurt Sauce:** Add ¼ cup (12 g) finely chopped fresh herbs (basil, cilantro, dill, mint, parsley, tarragon)
- **Lemon Yogurt Sauce:** Swap the water with freshly squeezed lemon juice
- **Spicy Yogurt Sauce:** Add 1 to 2 tablespoons (15 to 30 ml) Sriracha
- **Yogurt Ranch Sauce:** Use half water and half freshly squeezed lemon juice, and add 2 tablespoons (6 g) finely chopped parsley and 2 tablespoons (6 g) snipped chives
- **Harissa Yogurt Sauce:** Add 1 tablespoon (6 g) harissa

**Makes about 1 cup (235 ml)**

1 cup (240 g) plain Greek yogurt
¼ cup (60 ml) water
1 tablespoon (15 ml) extra-virgin olive oil
1 clove garlic, minced
Kosher salt and freshly ground black pepper

**Note:** The sauce can be stored in an airtight container in the refrigerator for up to 4 days.

**Try It Here!**
- Crispy Potato and Smoked Salmon Power Bowls, page 51
- Moroccan Salmon and Millet Bowls, page 61
- BBQ Chicken Quinoa Bowls, page 86
- Chicken Kofta Bowls, page 92
- Banh Mi Bowls, page 128
- Za'atar Chickpea Bowls, page 120
- Turmeric-Roasted Vegetable Bowls, page 153
- Masala Chickpea Bowls, page 140
- Moroccan-Spiced Chickpea Bowls, page 146

# Breakfast
# BOWLS

Coconut Quinoa Breakfast Bowls **30**

Apple Pie Farro Breakfast Bowls **31**

Blackberry Millet Breakfast Bowls **32**

Maple-Vanilla Overnight Oat Bowls **34**

Pomegranate and Freekeh Breakfast Tabbouleh Bowls **35**

Maple-Masala Winter Squash Breakfast Bowls **37**

Chai-Spiced Multigrain Porridge Bowls **38**

Sweet Potato Breakfast Bowls **39**

Slow Cooker Miso Oat and Egg Bowls **40**

Golden Milk Chia Seed Breakfast Bowls **42**

Vitamin C Papaya Bowls **43**

Spinach and Mushroom Pesto Breakfast Bowls **44**

Black Bean and Chorizo Bowls **46**

Slow Cooker Congee Breakfast Bowls **47**

Buckwheat and Black Bean Breakfast Bowls **48**

Scrambled Chickpea Breakfast Bowls **49**

Crispy Potato and Smoked Salmon Power Bowls **51**

Tofu Scramble Bowls with Kale and Brussels Sprouts **52**

# Coconut Quinoa Breakfast Bowls

Calling all coconut lovers! Packed with protein, good fats, and a triple dose of coconut, this is a wholesome, filling breakfast guaranteed to power you through the morning. While any type of quinoa works well here, red or black quinoa (or even a mix of the two) are my favorite choice for this bowl. Both varieties lend a deeper flavor with earthier, nuttier undertones that prove a nice contrast to the richness of the coconut milk and sweetness of the fruit. Take the extra couple of minutes to toast the quinoa first—you'll be so glad you did. If you're new to cooking red or black quinoa, you will also notice that it takes a touch longer to cook than white quinoa.

VEGETARIAN · GLUTEN FREE

**Serves 4**

1 tablespoon (14 g) coconut oil
1½ cups (265 g) red or black quinoa, rinsed
1 (14-ounce, or 392 g) can unsweetened light coconut milk, plus more for serving
2 cups (470 ml) water
Fine sea salt
2 tablespoons (40 g) honey, agave, or maple syrup
2 teaspoons (10 ml) vanilla extract
Coconut yogurt
Blueberries
Goji berries
Toasted pumpkin seeds
Toasted unsweetened coconut flakes

1 Heat the oil in a saucepan over medium heat. Add the quinoa and toast for about 2 minutes, stirring frequently. Slowly stir in the can of coconut milk, the water, and a pinch of salt. The quinoa will bubble and spurt at first but will quickly settle. Bring to a boil, then cover, reduce the heat to low, and simmer until it reaches a tender, creamy consistency, about 20 minutes. Remove from the heat and stir in the honey, agave, or maple syrup and vanilla.

2 To serve, divide the quinoa among bowls. Top with extra coconut milk, coconut yogurt, blueberries, goji berries, pumpkin seeds, and coconut flakes.

**What's the Difference Between White, Red, and Black Quinoa?**
For starters, all three varieties are equals when it comes to health and nutrition. Each one is gluten free, is a complete protein, and boasts a good dose of fiber and iron. There are a couple of subtle differences that set them apart: cook time, chewiness, and flavor. White quinoa has the mildest flavor of the three and generally takes about 15 minutes to cook. Red quinoa requires a few extra minutes on the stove, comes with a nuttier flavor, and has slightly more chew, while black quinoa is the nuttiest of the three, with the most distinct flavor and texture, and benefits from an extra 5 minutes of cook time. They can all be used interchangeably, so the one you choose all comes down to personal preference.

# Apple Pie Farro Breakfast Bowls

On chilly fall and winter mornings, there are few things I find more comforting and nourishing than cozying up with this warm fruit and nut-filled bowl (paired with a steaming mug of coffee, of course!). Chopped apple and a medley of spices are cooked alongside the farro, for a wholesome result that will remind you of the warm notes of apple pie. Take your pick between sweet or tart apples, both work wonderfully, though do use firm apples, like Cortland, Honeycrisp, or Granny Smith. These varieties hold their shape best during cooking—they'll soften just enough, without becoming mushy and totally falling apart. If you choose to get a head start on making the farro before morning, hold off on adding the toppings until right before serving.

1 Add one of the chopped apples, along with the farro, water, milk, cinnamon, ginger, allspice, and a pinch of salt to a medium saucepan, and stir together. Bring to a boil. Reduce the heat to low, cover, and simmer, stirring occasionally, until tender, 30 to 35 minutes. All of the liquid will not be absorbed. Remove from the heat, stir in the maple syrup, honey, or agave and vanilla, then cover and steam for 5 minutes.

2 To serve, divide the farro among bowls. Add the remaining apple and top with pecans, raisins, pumpkin seeds, and hemp seeds.

VEGETARIAN | **Serves 4**

2 apples, chopped, divided
1 cup (165 g) pearled farro
4 cups (940 ml) water
1½ cups (355 ml) milk (dairy or nondairy)
1 teaspoon (2 g) ground cinnamon
½ teaspoon ground ginger
⅛ teaspoon allspice
Fine sea salt
2 tablespoons (30 ml) maple syrup, honey, or agave
½ teaspoon vanilla extract
Toasted pecans
Raisins
Toasted pumpkin seeds
Hemp seeds

# Blackberry Millet Breakfast Bowls

If you have a thing for steel-cut oats, you should really give this millet bowl a try. While the grains are slightly smaller, millet retains that firm, chewy texture similar to steel-cut oats, though it cooks in a fraction of the time. I love fresh fruit as a topping for breakfast bowls, and here I take it one step further by cooking a handful of berries with the millet. As they simmer, the berries break down and infuse their jammy, sweet flavor through the grains.

If blackberries aren't in season or prove tricky to find, go ahead and swap in raspberries, chopped strawberries, blueberries, or even a mixture. They work just as well and make for a delicious breakfast. If you make the millet in advance, hold off on adding the yogurt and toppings until serving.

**VEGETARIAN · GLUTEN FREE**

**Serves 4**

1 cup (165 g) uncooked millet
2 cups (470 ml) milk (dairy or nondairy)
1½ cups (355 ml) water
1½ cups (220 g) blackberries, divided
½ teaspoon ground ginger
Fine sea salt
3 tablespoons (60 g) honey, plus more for topping
1 teaspoon (5 ml) vanilla extract
2 tablespoons (30 ml) freshly squeezed lemon juice
1 cup (240 g) plain Greek yogurt
Toasted walnuts, chopped
Unsweetened toasted coconut flakes

1 Combine the millet, milk, water, ½ cup (75 g) of the berries, ginger, and a pinch of salt in a medium saucepan. Bring to a boil, then reduce the heat to low, cover, and simmer until tender but not all the liquid has been absorbed, about 15 minutes. Stir occasionally and break up the berries with a spoon as they soften. Remove from the heat and steam with the lid on for 5 minutes. Stir in the honey and vanilla.

2 Meanwhile, whisk the lemon juice into the yogurt.

3 To serve, divide the millet among bowls. Top with yogurt mixture, the remaining 1 cup (145 g) blackberries, walnuts, coconut, and a drizzle of honey.

# Maple-Vanilla Overnight Oat Bowls

Oats are one of those breakfasts I can eat day in and day out and never get tired of, particularly chilled overnight oats. While these bowls require some forethought and advance planning, the result is a tiny gift to your future self. Mix up the oats in the evening, let them soak in the fridge overnight, and breakfast is waiting for you when you wake up. Subtly sweet maple and vanilla-scented oats, softened with milk and yogurt, are ready to be spooned into your favorite bowl and topped with a pile of fruit and nuts.

**VEGETARIAN · GLUTEN FREE**

**Serves 4**

1½ cups (355 ml) milk (dairy or
    nondairy)
1 cup (240 g) plain or vanilla Greek
    yogurt
3 tablespoons (45 ml) maple syrup
2 teaspoons (10 ml) vanilla extract
1½ cups (120 g) old-fashioned oats
3 tablespoons (18 g) chia seeds
1 banana, sliced
4 fresh figs, quartered
Chopped pistachios
Nut butter

1 Whisk together the milk, yogurt, maple syrup, and vanilla in a large bowl. Add the oats and chia seeds; stir to combine. Cover and refrigerate overnight.

2 To serve, stir the oat mixture together and divide among bowls. Top with banana, figs, and pistachios. Drizzle with nut butter.

# Pomegranate and Freekeh Breakfast Tabbouleh Bowls

One of my favorites ways to keep my meals interesting without finding new recipes all the time is taking a familiar recipe—in this case, classic tabbouleh salad—and reinventing it with a totally new set of flavors or textures. Here, the savory Middle Eastern salad becomes breakfast fare with a sweet, fresh twist by swapping vegetables for crisp apple and pomegranate, while fresh mint replaces parsley. A healthy scoop of orange blossom–scented Greek yogurt finishes off the bowls with a beautiful fragrance and an extra punch of protein to make it more filling.

This bowl is best served chilled or at room temperature, and when you prep all the components in advance, all that's left to do before sitting down to breakfast is to assemble the bowls.

**VEGETARIAN** | **Serves 4**

¾ cup (125 g) cracked freekeh
2 cups (470 ml) water
Fine sea salt and freshly ground black pepper
1 crisp apple, cored and diced, divided
1 cup (120 g) pomegranate arils
½ cup (24 g) chopped fresh mint
1 tablespoon (15 ml) extra-virgin olive oil
1½ tablespoons (23 ml) orange blossom water
2 cups (480 g) plain Greek yogurt
Roasted unsalted almonds, chopped

1 Combine the freekeh, water, and a pinch of salt in a medium saucepan. Bring to a boil, then reduce the heat to low and simmer for 15 minutes, stirring occasionally, until all the liquid has been absorbed and the freekeh is tender. Remove from the heat, cover with a lid, and steam for about 5 minutes. Transfer the freekeh to a bowl and cool completely.

2 Add half of the apple and the pomegranate, mint, olive oil, and a couple grinds of pepper to the freekeh and stir well to combine.

3 Stir the orange blossom water into the yogurt until well combined.

4 To serve, divide the freekeh among bowls. Top with the orange-scented yogurt, remaining apple, and almonds.

# Maple-Masala Winter Squash Breakfast Bowls

For anyone who loves the sweet warmth of maple-cinnamon roasted winter squash, this breakfast bowl brings a fun, flavorful twist that you're going to love! There's no cinnamon to be found in this recipe (at least not directly); instead, a sprinkle of garam masala, the warm and fragrant Indian spice blend typically combining cinnamon, cloves, coriander, cardamom, and pepper, is partnered with maple syrup and coconut oil, and brings a much deeper spiced flavor than cinnamon alone. The other thing you will love about this recipe is that acorn squash is just the right size to serve as both the heart of your meal and the bowl itself. Once it's roasted and cooled slightly, each half is filled with protein-rich Greek yogurt and a colorful mix of crunchy and chewy healthy toppings.

1 Preheat the oven to 375°F (190°C, or gas mark 5).

2 Slice the squash in half from stem to bottom. Scoop out and discard the seeds. Brush the flesh of each half with oil and maple syrup, then sprinkle with garam masala and a pinch of sea salt. Place the squash on a rimmed baking sheet cut-side down. Bake until soft, 35 to 40 minutes.

3 Turn the squash over and cool slightly.

4 To serve, fill each squash half with yogurt and granola. Top with goji berries, pomegranate arils, pecans, and pumpkin seeds, drizzle with nut butter, and sprinkle with hemp seeds.

VEGETARIAN · GLUTEN FREE

**Serves 4**

2 medium acorn squash
4 teaspoons (20 g) coconut oil
1 tablespoon (15 ml) maple syrup or brown sugar
1 teaspoon (2 g) garam masala
Fine sea salt
2 cups (480 g) plain Greek yogurt
Granola
Goji berries
Pomegranate arils
Chopped pecans
Toasted pumpkin seeds
Nut butter
Hemp seeds

# Chai-Spiced Multigrain Porridge Bowls

Fresh off a long flight from New York to Sydney, Australia, I let my friend Sarah usher me straight from the airport to a corner breakfast spot in her neighborhood called the Driftwood Cafe. Who was I to argue? We were sitting beachside, it was sunny and 40 degrees warmer than when I left New York, and she was certain I'd love the chill vibe along with everything on the menu. That was the morning I fell head over heels for the warm, spiced notes and pure sense of comfort that come with chai tea. And those are the very same qualities that come through with each bite of these breakfast bowls that combine steel-cut oats, barley, and quinoa for maximum texture.

VEGETARIAN | **Serves 4**

2 cups (470 ml) water
3 chai tea bags
⅓ cup (26 g) steel-cut oats
⅓ cup (55 g) pearled barley
⅓ cup (60 g) quinoa, rinsed
Fine sea salt
1½ cups (355 ml) milk (dairy or
   nondairy)
3 tablespoons (60 g) honey, maple
   syrup, or agave
1 teaspoon (5 ml) vanilla extract
1 banana, sliced
Unsweetened toasted coconut flakes
Cacao nibs
Toasted pecans

1 Bring the water to a boil in a medium saucepan. Remove from the heat, add the tea bags, and steep for 5 minutes. Remove and discard the tea bags.

2 Return the pan to low heat and add the oats, barley, quinoa, and a pinch of salt. Cook, stirring occasionally and scraping the bottom of the pan as necessary, until most but not all of the water is absorbed, about 15 minutes. Slowly stir in the milk. Continue cooking, stirring occasionally, until the grains are tender and creamy, about 20 minutes longer. Remove from the heat and stir in the honey, maple syrup, or agave and vanilla.

3 To serve, divide the porridge among bowls. Top with banana, coconut, cacao nibs, and pecans.

# Sweet Potato Breakfast Bowls

Every week, without fail, I always bake a few sweet potatoes during my Sunday meal prep. Having them in the fridge means a quick addition to salads, tacos, savory bowls, and, best of all, a quick breakfast bowl. You can certainly serve this breakfast chilled, though I think it's as its best when gently warmed. That's when the ghee and almond butter (my nut butter of choice) gently melt into the lush folds of the mashed potato.

1 Gently warm the sweet potatoes. Peel and mash well with a fork in a large bowl. Add the nut butter, ghee, and cinnamon, and stir well to combine.

2 Divide the mashed sweet potato among bowls. Top with sliced bananas, blueberries, strawberries, almonds, hemp seeds, and an extra drizzle of nut butter.

VEGAN · GLUTEN FREE

**Serves 4**

2 large or 4 small sweet potatoes, baked

¼ cup (65 g) creamy nut butter, plus more for drizzling

1 tablespoon (14 g) ghee

½ teaspoon ground cinnamon

1 banana, sliced

Fresh blueberries

Chopped strawberries

Sliced almonds

Hemp seeds

# Slow Cooker Miso Oat and Egg Bowls

If you have yet to get acquainted with the savory side of steel-cut oats, there is no time like the present to make it happen. And with your slow cooker leading the charge, these warming break-fast bowls could not be easier to get on the table. Full-flavored broth replaces water for cooking and a spoonful of miso paste whisked in at the end is what takes it over the top. This recipe calls for sweet white miso, which I love for its delicate, umami-rich flavor and the way it makes a humble bowl of oats taste totally indulgent, though feel free to experiment with other varieties of miso. A soft-cooked egg with a lush, jammy center is the ultimate pairing for these savory oats, while radishes and sprouts offer a balance of freshness.

**VEGETARIAN | Serves 4**

1 cup (80 g) steel-cut oats
4 cups (940 ml) vegetable or chicken broth
3 tablespoons (45 g) white miso
1 tablespoon (14 g) unsalted butter, plus more for greasing the slow cooker
4 large eggs
4 radishes, thinly sliced
Broccoli, clover, or alfalfa sprouts
Toasted pumpkin seeds

**Cooking Tip!** Don't skip the ice bath when making boiled eggs. The benefits are twofold: The cold water stops the eggs from cooking any further and it makes them much easier to peel.

1 Thoroughly coat the insert of a 6-quart (5.4 L) or larger slow cooker with a light layer of butter. Combine the oats and broth in the insert and stir together. Cover and cook on low for 7 to 8 hours.

2 Stir the oats together once more. Whisk the miso and butter into the oats. Keep the slow cooker on warm while you prepare the eggs.

3 Bring a medium saucepan of water to a boil over medium heat. Use a spoon to carefully lower the eggs into the water. Cook for 6 minutes, maintaining a gentle boil. Reduce the heat if necessary. Transfer the eggs to an ice bath, until they're cool enough to handle but still warm. Peel the eggs, and slice each one in half.

4 To serve, divide the oats among bowls. Top with an egg, sliced radish, sprouts, and pumpkin seeds.

# Golden Milk Chia Seed Breakfast Bowls

By now, even if you're not drinking it, I'm sure you've heard of golden milk, the warm, electric-yellow beverage blended with turmeric and a slew of spices. It's a staple among the wellness set, myself included, and feels blissfully calming and soothing. Here, it's the base for a nourishing chia pudding, topped with fresh fruits, nuts, and seeds, that I love eating for breakfast (as well as a snack and dessert).

Don't skip the coconut oil. Along with the cashew milk, it adds a dose of healthy fat to your breakfast bowl, and more importantly helps our bodies absorb fat-soluble turmeric. Think of it as your insurance policy for getting that nourishing, anti-inflammatory boost for which turmeric is so well known.

VEGAN · GLUTEN FREE

**Serves 4**

4 cups (940 ml) unsweetened cashew milk
1 tablespoon (14 g) coconut oil
1 teaspoon (2 g) ground turmeric
¼ teaspoon ground ginger
¼ teaspoon ground cinnamon
¼ teaspoon fine sea salt
⅛ teaspoon ground cardamom
6 pitted dates
1 teaspoon (5 ml) vanilla extract
¾ cup (72 g) chia seeds
Blueberries
Fresh figs, quartered
Unsweetened toasted coconut flakes
Sliced almonds
Hemp seeds

1 Add the milk, coconut oil, turmeric, ginger, cinnamon, salt, and cardamom to a medium saucepan. Whisk together and simmer over medium-low heat until warm and the spices are well combined. Do not bring to a boil. Remove from the heat and cool for about 10 minutes.

2 Transfer the milk to a blender along with the dates and vanilla. Blend continuously at high speed until the dates are completely broken down and the liquid is smooth. Add the chia seeds and blend just until combined. Pour into a large bowl, cover, and refrigerate for at least 6 hours or overnight to thicken.

3 To serve, divide the chia pudding among bowls. Top with blueberries, fresh figs, coconut flakes, almonds, and hemp seeds.

# Vitamin C Papaya Bowls

If yogurt and fruit is your breakfast go-to, consider this bowl a fun way to jazz up the mornings. When it comes to loading up on immunity-boosting, anti-inflammatory vitamin C, tropical papaya tops the charts. Yes, even more than citrus. When cut in half, these oblong fruits can also double as a breakfast bowl.

Making the popped amaranth is quite easy, though it can take a batch or two to get the hang of it. A screaming-hot pot is essential, and the best way to know when it's ready is by dropping in a few grains of amaranth. They should pop almost instantly, which is your signal that the pot is hot enough. If they don't pop right away, give the pot another minute to heat up, and test again. Also, do keep a lid over the pot, or you'll have quite the mess on your stovetop.

1 Heat a tall, wide saucepan over medium-high heat for several minutes. Check if the pan is hot enough by adding a few grains of amaranth. They should quiver and pop within a few seconds. If not, heat the pan for a minute longer and test again. When the pan is hot enough, add 1 tablespoon (10 g) of the amaranth. The grains should begin to pop within a few seconds. Cover the pot and shake occasionally, until all the grains are popped. Pour the popped amaranth into a bowl, and repeat with the remaining amaranth, 1 tablespoon (10 g) at a time.

2 Cut the papayas in half lengthwise, from stem to tail, then remove and discard the seeds. Fill each half with popped amaranth and coconut yogurt. Top with kiwi, grapefruit and orange segments, and sprinkle with hemp seeds and sesame seeds.

VEGAN · GLUTEN FREE

**Serves 4**

4 tablespoons (40 g) amaranth, divided
2 small ripe papayas (about 1 pound, or 455 g each)
2 cups (480 g) coconut yogurt
2 kiwis, peeled and diced
1 large pink grapefruit, peeled and segmented
1 large navel orange, peeled and segmented
Hemp seeds
Black sesame seeds

# Spinach and Mushroom Pesto Breakfast Bowls

In my old New York City neighborhood there was a breakfast joint called The Barking Dog that, among many things, introduced me to the coupling of eggs with fresh, herby pesto sauce and earthy mushrooms. It's been years since I've been there, but that menu item left a lasting impression and most recently is the inspiration for this veggie-filled breakfast bowl.

While I suggest basil pesto with this bowl combination, feel free to make it with any of your favorite herbs. Even greens like arugula or kale would make a fine choice. Pesto is a great sauce to make in advance and stash in the freezer, so you always have some on hand. Even the mushrooms and spinach can be sautéed ahead of time, then reheated or simply added to the bowl chilled.

VEGETARIAN · GLUTEN FREE

**Serves 4**

3 tablespoons (45 ml) avocado or
    extra-virgin olive oil, divided
16 cremini mushrooms, quartered
Kosher salt and freshly ground
    pepper
8 packed cups (240 g) baby spinach
4 large eggs
8 ounces (225 g) zucchini noodles
½ cup (120 ml) Basil Pesto Sauce
    (page 21)
2 avocados, peeled, pitted, and diced
Red pepper flakes

1 Heat 1 tablespoon (15 ml) of the oil in a large skillet over medium-high heat. Add the mushrooms and season with salt and pepper. Cook, stirring occasionally, until well browned, about 5 minutes. Transfer to a plate and set aside.

2 Heat another tablespoon (15 ml) of oil in the same pan over medium heat. Add the spinach. Cook, tossing occasionally, until wilted, about 2 minutes. Transfer to the plate with the mushrooms. Heat the remaining 1 tablespoon (15 ml) oil in the skillet and fry the eggs.

3 Toss the zucchini noodles with a spoonful of pesto. To serve, divide the zucchini noodles among bowls. Add the mushrooms, spinach, fried egg, and avocado. Top with extra pesto and sprinkle with red pepper flakes.

# Black Bean and Chorizo Bowls

Breakfast burritos are my weakness. I simply cannot resist that combination of eggs, crumbled, smoky meat, beans, and salsa rolled into a savory package. They are undeniably delicious and I can always be certain they'll fill me up. These bowls are inspired by everything there is to love about a really good breakfast burrito, with a healthier spin.

Because I believe a helping (or two!) of vegetables in the morning is always a good idea, these bowls start off with a bed of cilantro-flecked cauliflower rice. Traditional scrambled eggs are swapped for a runny-yolk fried egg, then partnered with lightly spiced and smoky chorizo crumbles, hearty black beans, and a pop of freshness from a handful of baby spinach. And of course, no breakfast burrito bowl would be complete without salsa. Classic tomato salsa or salsa verde are my top picks to finish off your bowl. Get a head start by cooking the chorizo and cauliflower rice ahead of time, then reheat just before serving, while you make the fried eggs.

GLUTEN FREE | **Serves 4**

3 cups (90 g) baby spinach
2 tablespoons (30 ml) avocado or
   extra-virgin olive oil, divided
8 ounces (225 g) riced cauliflower
Kosher salt and freshly ground black
   pepper
¼ cup (4 g) finely chopped fresh
   cilantro, plus more for topping
8 ounces (225 g) Mexican chorizo or
   soyrizo, casings removed
4 large eggs
1 cup (200 g) black beans, drained
   and rinsed
Salsa
½ cup (120 ml) Avocado Sauce
   (page 17)

1 Divide the spinach among bowls.

2 Heat 1 tablespoon (15 ml) of the oil in a large skillet over medium heat. Add the riced cauliflower and season with salt and pepper. Cook, stirring occasionally, until the cauliflower is heated through and slightly softened, about 3 minutes. Remove from the heat and stir in the cilantro. Divide among the bowls. Wipe the pan clean.

3 Heat the remaining 1 tablespoon (15 ml) oil in the same pan over medium heat. Add the chorizo. Cook, breaking up the meat with a wooden spoon, until cooked through and well browned, 6 to 8 minutes. Use a slotted spoon to transfer the chorizo to a paper towel–lined plate.

4 Reduce the heat to low and fry the eggs in the same pan.

5 To serve, top the bowls with chorizo, egg, black beans, and salsa. Drizzle with Avocado Sauce and sprinkle with extra cilantro.

# Slow Cooker Congee Breakfast Bowls

Looking back to my childhood, there are few breakfasts I remember quite as fondly as steaming hot bowls of cream of wheat or cream of rice. Even now, just thinking about them makes my belly feel warm and full of comfort. If you share the same fondness for hot, creamy breakfast cereal, congee will be right up your alley. It's a simple, ultra-comforting, and nourishing rice porridge that cooks low and slow until the grains of rice break down and become creamy. Here, it's infused with a few coins of fresh ginger and a few cups of stock for a more savory flavor. In the time it takes my coffee to brew, I can give the vegetables a quick sauté and fry a couple of eggs. A note on kimchi: Many traditional versions contain shellfish products, so if you're avoiding shellfish, look for a jar of vegetarian or vegan kimchi.

1 Add the rice, water, stock, ginger, and 1 teaspoon (6 g) salt to a 3½-quart (3.2 L) or larger slow cooker and stir together. Cover, set to low, and cook until the rice is broken down and creamy, about 8 hours.

2 Remove and discard the ginger. Stir, scraping the sides and bottom of the slow cooker. Divide the congee among bowls.

3 Heat 1 tablespoon (15 ml) of the oil in a large skillet over medium-high heat. Add the mushrooms, season with salt and pepper, and sauté until tender, about 5 minutes. Spoon over the congee.

4 Heat 1 tablespoon (15 ml) of oil in the same skillet over medium heat. Add the spinach and cook, tossing occasionally, until just wilted, about 2 minutes. Divide the spinach among the bowls.

5 Heat the remaining 1 tablespoon (15 ml) oil in the same skillet, and fry the eggs.

6 Add the eggs to the bowls of congee, and top with kimchi and scallions.

VEGETARIAN · GLUTEN FREE

**Serves 4**

¾ cup (125 g) jasmine rice

4 cups (940 ml) water

3 cups (705 ml) vegetable or chicken stock

1-inch (2.5 cm) piece fresh ginger, peeled and thinly sliced

Kosher salt and freshly ground black pepper

3 tablespoons (45 ml) avocado or extra-virgin olive oil, divided

6 ounces (168 g) mushrooms, preferably cremini or shiitake, sliced

6 cups (180 g) baby spinach

4 large eggs

Kimchi

Scallions, thinly sliced

# Buckwheat and Black Bean Breakfast Bowls

This bowl is my attempt at breaking away from yet another morning of avocado toast topped with a rushed, lacy-edged fried egg and a scattering of crumbled cheese or vegetables. You can see I haven't exactly stepped very far, and that's just fine by me. While I've traded the toast for some lightly buttered, nutty buckwheat, this bowl is a gathering of all my favorite avocado toast toppings, like dark leafy greens, protein-rich beans, briny feta crumbles, and a dash of heat. But unlike avocado toast, this breakfast can be prepped entirely ahead of time, so all that's left to do in the morning is mash the avocado and pile everything into your favorite bowl.

**VEGETARIAN · GLUTEN FREE**

**Serves 4**

¾ cup (125 g) kasha buckwheat
1⅓ cups (315 ml) water
½ tablespoon (7 g) unsalted butter
Kosher salt and freshly ground black pepper
4 cups (520 g) steamed kale
1½ cups (300 g) or 1 (15-ounce, or 420 g) can black beans, drained and rinsed
4 hard-boiled eggs
2 avocados, peeled, pitted, and mashed
1 watermelon radish, thinly sliced
Crumbled feta
1 recipe Miso-Ginger Sauce (page 23)
Sesame seeds
Aleppo pepper

1 Combine the buckwheat, water, butter, and a generous pinch of salt in a medium saucepan. Bring to a boil, then reduce the heat to low, cover, and simmer until tender, 15 to 20 minutes.

2 To serve, divide the buckwheat among bowls. Top with the steamed kale, beans, sliced hard-boiled egg, avocado, radish, and feta. Drizzle with Miso-Ginger Sauce and sprinkle with sesame seeds and Aleppo pepper.

# Scrambled Chickpea Breakfast Bowls

If you skew toward all things savory when it comes to breakfast, then this vegan scramble will be right up your alley. I first made a version of this cumin and turmeric–spiced chickpea scramble as a breakfast wrap and was instantly smitten. So, it was without hesitation that I turned it into a loaded bowl, packed with even more veggies and an herb-flecked tahini sauce to bring it all together.

All of the components in this chickpea bowl can be made in advance, and then reheated or simply piled into a bowl straight from the fridge when you're ready to serve.

1 Divide the spinach among bowls.

2 Heat 1 tablespoon (15 ml) of the oil in a large, high-sided skillet over medium heat. Add the riced cauliflower and season with salt and pepper. Cook, stirring occasionally, until tender, about 3 minutes. Spoon over the spinach.

3 Heat the remaining 2 tablespoons (30 ml) oil in the same skillet over medium heat. Add the onion, bell pepper, salt, and pepper. Cook, stirring occasionally, until soft and fragrant, about 5 minutes. Meanwhile, mash half of the chickpeas with a fork. Stir in the whole and mashed chickpeas, garlic, cumin, coriander, and turmeric, and cook, stirring occasionally until soft, about 3 minutes.

4 To serve, top the spinach and riced cauliflower with the chickpeas and avocado. Drizzle with Green Tahini Sauce.

**VEGAN · GLUTEN FREE**

**Serves 4**

2 packed cups (60 g) baby spinach
3 tablespoons (45 ml) avocado or
    extra-virgin olive oil, divided
8 ounces (225 g) riced cauliflower
Kosher salt and freshly ground black
    pepper
½ medium onion, diced
1 red bell pepper, cored and diced
3 cups (600 g) or 2 (15-ounce, or
    420 g) cans chickpeas, drained
    and rinsed
1 clove garlic, minced
2 teaspoons (4 g) ground cumin
1 teaspoon (2 g) ground coriander
1 teaspoon (2 g) turmeric
2 avocados, peeled, pitted, and thinly
    sliced
1 recipe Green Tahini Sauce (page 26)

# Crispy Potato and Smoked Salmon Power Bowls

With smoked salmon and red onion, poached eggs, greens, and crispy potatoes, gilded in a lemony sauce, this recipe brings together some quintessential New York brunch foods in a single bowl. And while not commonly paired together as they are here, each one plays off the other in such a harmonious and delicious way. This is a bowl I would happily start my morning with, any day of the week, and particularly if I had company or was hosting weekend brunch.

1 Arrange an oven rack about 6 inches (15 cm) below the broiler, and set the oven to broil. Toss the potatoes and onion with 1 tablespoon (15 ml) of the oil, salt, and pepper. Arrange in a single layer on a rimmed baking sheet. Broil until browned and crisp around the edges, about 8 minutes.

2 Heat the remaining 1 tablespoon (15 ml) oil in a large skillet over medium heat until shimmering. Add the spinach and a pinch of salt. Cook, tossing occasionally, until wilted, 2 to 3 minutes.

3 To serve, divide the potatoes, onions, and spinach among bowls. Top with smoked salmon, a poached egg, cucumber, and avocado. Drizzle with Lemon Yogurt Sauce and sprinkle with fresh dill.

GLUTEN FREE | **Serves 4**

8 fingerling potatoes, halved lengthwise
1 medium red onion, cut into large pieces
2 tablespoons (30 ml) avocado or extra-virgin olive oil, divided
Kosher salt and freshly ground black pepper
6 packed cups (180 g) baby spinach
8 ounces (225 g) thinly sliced smoked salmon
4 poached eggs
½ medium English cucumber, halved and thinly sliced
1 avocado, peeled, pitted, and diced
1 recipe Lemon Yogurt Sauce (page 27)
Fresh dill

# Tofu Scramble Bowls with Kale and Brussels Sprouts

Despite the fact that I'm crazy about eggs in all forms, I like to change up my breakfast routine with tofu scrambles once in a while. The soft, creamy tofu curds have a consistency that's quite similar to scrambled eggs, and a dash of turmeric and nutritional yeast impart a golden hue and savory flavor. If you're used to roasting or sautéing Brussels sprouts, know that they can also be eaten raw and they're quite good this way. When buying them loose, stick with smaller sprouts because they have a milder taste than their larger counterparts.

**VEGAN · GLUTEN FREE**

**Serves 4**

2 cups (140 g) finely shredded Tuscan kale

½ pound (224 g) Brussels sprouts, trimmed and shredded

2½ tablespoons (37 ml) avocado or extra-virgin olive oil, divided

Juice from ½ lemon

Kosher salt and freshly ground black pepper

1 large sweet potato, cut into wedges

½ teaspoon paprika

14 ounces (392 g) extra-firm tofu, pressed and drained

3 scallions, white and green parts, thinly sliced

2 tablespoons (6 g) nutritional yeast

1 teaspoon (2 g) ground turmeric

½ teaspoon garlic powder

2 avocados, peeled, pitted, and thinly sliced

1 recipe Green Tahini Sauce (page 26)

Sunflower seeds

1 Preheat the oven to 425°F (220°C, or gas mark 7).

2 Add the kale and Brussels sprouts to a large bowl. Rub with ½ tablespoon (7 ml) of the oil and toss with the lemon juice and a pinch of salt; set aside.

3 Add the potato wedges to a rimmed baking sheet and toss with 1 tablespoon (15 ml) of oil, paprika, salt, and pepper. Roast until tender and lightly browned, about 20 minutes, stirring once halfway through. Meanwhile, prepare the tofu.

4 Add the tofu to a medium bowl, and break into small curds with a fork or your fingers. Heat the remaining 1 tablespoon (15 ml) oil in a large skillet over medium-high heat. Add the scallions and sauté until soft and fragrant, about 2 minutes. Add the tofu and sauté for 2 minutes. Add the nutritional yeast, turmeric, garlic powder, salt, and pepper, and stir until well combined. Continue cooking until the tofu is heated through and lightly browned, 4 to 5 minutes longer.

5 To serve, divide the kale and Brussels sprouts among bowls. Top with roasted sweet potato, scrambled tofu, and avocado, then drizzle with Green Tahini Sauce and sprinkle with sunflower seeds.

# Fish and Seafood BOWLS

Lentil and Smoked Salmon Niçoise Bowls **56**

Almond-Quinoa and Salmon Bowls **57**

Smoked Salmon and Soba Noodle Bowls **58**

Moroccan Salmon and Millet Bowls **61**

Bittersweet Citrus and Salmon Power Bowls **62**

Salmon Teriyaki Bowls with Miso-Braised Kale **64**

Tomato-Braised Cod and Barley Bowls **65**

Sesame Tuna Bowls **66**

Shrimp Summer Roll Bowls **69**

Vietnamese Zucchini Noodle and Shrimp Bowls **70**

Balsamic Shrimp and Farro Bowls **72**

Freekeh Bowls with Caramelized Onions, Warm Tomatoes, and Seared Fish **73**

Superfood Salmon Bowls **74**

Brown Rice Bowls with Seared Fish and Chimichurri **75**

# Lentil and Smoked Salmon Niçoise Bowls

It wasn't until I met my husband that I really fell in love with smoked salmon. He ate it often, usually with its silky folds piled on a water cracker with a generous squeeze of fresh lemon juice, and through him I came to appreciate its luxurious richness. These days I take any and all opportunities to work it into meals, especially lunch bowls, which is why taking apart a classic Niçoise salad and turning it into a Buddha bowl, with smoked salmon leading the charge, felt like a no-brainer.

GLUTEN FREE | **Serves 4**

¾ cup (144 g) French lentils
Kosher salt and freshly ground black pepper
8 fingerling potatoes, halved lengthwise
2 tablespoons (30 ml) avocado or extra-virgin olive oil, divided
1 shallot, diced
6 ounces (168 g) green beans, trimmed
2 packed cups (40 g) arugula
1 cup (150 g) grape tomatoes, halved
8 radishes, quartered
1 bulb fennel, trimmed and thinly sliced
4 hard-boiled eggs, halved
4 ounces (115 g) thinly sliced smoked salmon
1 recipe White Wine–Lemon Vinaigrette (page 18)

1 Preheat the oven to 425°F (220°C, or gas mark 7).

2 Add the lentils and a generous pinch of salt to a medium saucepan, and cover with water by at least 2 inches (5 cm). Bring to a boil, then reduce the heat to low and simmer until tender, about 25 minutes. Drain the excess water.

3 Toss the potatoes with 1 tablespoon (15 ml) of the oil, salt, and pepper. Arrange in a single layer on a rimmed baking sheet. Roast until tender and lightly browned, about 20 minutes. Set aside.

4 Meanwhile, heat the remaining 1 tablespoon (15 ml) oil in a skillet over medium heat. Sauté the shallot until soft, about 3 minutes. Add the green beans and season with salt and pepper. Cook, stirring occasionally, until just tender, about 5 minutes.

5 To serve, divide the lentils and arugula among bowls. Top with crispy potatoes, green beans, tomatoes, radish, fennel, egg, and smoked salmon. Drizzle with White Wine–Lemon Vinaigrette.

# Almond-Quinoa and Salmon Bowls

Sometimes there is a single ingredient that takes all the credit for bringing a Buddha bowl to life. In this case, it's the Roasted Red Pepper Sauce. Inspired by romesco, a smoky red pepper and almond sauce that hails from Spain, this version is a true gem. It's creamy and rich, almost decadent, yet totally healthy and surprisingly easy to pull together in just minutes. Here, it accents the fatty salmon, tempers the bitter bite of broccolini and arugula, and makes a nice partner to the almond-studded quinoa, to really tie the whole bowl together.

1 Combine the quinoa, water, and a generous pinch of salt in a medium saucepan. Bring to a boil, then reduce the heat to a simmer and cook, uncovered, until tender, about 15 minutes. Remove from the heat, cover with a lid, and steam for about 5 minutes. Fluff the quinoa with a fork, and then stir in ½ tablespoon (7 ml) of the oil and the almonds.

2 Arrange an oven rack about 6 inches (15 cm) below the boiler, and set the oven to broil.

3 Arrange the salmon on one side of a rimmed baking sheet, skin-side down. Lightly brush with 1 tablespoon (15 ml) of the oil and season with salt and pepper. Toss the broccolini with the remaining 1 tablespoon (15 ml) oil, salt, and pepper. Spread the broccolini in a single layer on the other side of the baking sheet. Broil until the salmon is cooked through and flakes easily, 6 to 8 minutes, depending on thickness.

4 To serve, divide the quinoa among bowls. Top with salmon, broccolini, beets, and arugula. Drizzle with Roasted Red Pepper Sauce and sprinkle with almonds.

GLUTEN FREE | **Serves 4**

1 cup (175 g) quinoa, rinsed
2 cups (470 ml) water
Kosher salt and freshly ground black pepper
2½ tablespoons (37 ml) avocado or extra-virgin olive oil, divided
¼ cup (36 g) chopped toasted almonds, plus more for topping
4 (4- to 6-ounce, 115 to 168 g) salmon fillets
12 bunches broccolini
2 large beets, peeled and thinly sliced
2 cups (40 g) arugula
¾ cup (180 ml) Roasted Red Pepper Sauce (page 25)

# Smoked Salmon and Soba Noodle Bowls

While I've been eating smoked salmon for years, I didn't truly fall in love with it until I started adding it to noodle bowls, like this one. The silky, thin layers of this cured fish come with a fatty richness that take a simple bowl from good to great. It balances the nuttiness of the soba noodles and bright freshness of the vegetables with a hint of wholesome indulgence that make a mid-week meal feel a little more special. What's not to love about that? One thing to remember is that soba noodles have a tendency to stick and clump together, so be sure to rinse them well after cooking.

GLUTEN FREE | **Serves 4**

4 tablespoons (60 ml) tamari
1 tablespoon (15 ml) rice vinegar
1 tablespoon (6 g) freshly grated
   ginger
1 teaspoon (5 ml) toasted sesame oil
½ teaspoon honey
6 ounces (168 g) dry buckwheat soba
   noodles
1 cup (120 g) shelled edamame
4 ounces (115 g) thinly sliced smoked
   salmon
1 medium seedless cucumber, peeled
   and julienned
1 avocado, peeled, pitted, and thinly
   sliced
Shredded nori
Red pepper flakes

1 Whisk the tamari, rice vinegar, ginger, sesame oil, and honey together in a small bowl; set aside.

2 Bring a large pot of salted water to a boil. Cook the soba noodles according to the package instructions. Drain the noodles and rinse thoroughly with cold water. Stir the sauce together once more and toss the noodles with 1 tablespoon (15 ml) of sauce.

3 To serve, divide the soba noodles among bowls. Top with edamame, smoked salmon, cucumber, and avocado. Drizzle with sauce and sprinkle with nori and red pepper flakes.

# Moroccan Salmon and Millet Bowls

Salmon comes with a slew of health benefits (hello, omega-3s and B vitamins!) that make it a popular dinner choice in my house. Its quick cook time and versatility are just the icing on the cake. Here, salmon gets a Moroccan twist and a serious boost of flavor thanks to an earthy, smoky-sweet spice rub, before it's partnered with harissa-roasted carrots, herb-flecked millet, and a creamy yogurt sauce. If you want to get a head start, everything from the millet to the carrots, yogurt sauce, and even the salmon can all be made in advance.

1 Preheat the oven to 425°F (220°C, or gas mark 7).

2 Add the millet to a large, dry saucepan and toast over medium heat until golden brown, 4 to 5 minutes. Add the water and a generous pinch of salt. The water will sputter but will settle down quickly. Bring to a boil. Reduce the heat to low, stir in 1 tablespoon (15 ml) of the oil, cover, and simmer until most of the water is absorbed, 15 to 20 minutes. Remove from the heat and steam in the pot for 5 minutes. Once cooled, stir in the currants, mint, and parsley.

3 Meanwhile, peel and slice the carrots into ½-inch (1.3 cm)-thick rounds. Whisk together 1½ tablespoons (23 ml) of oil, harissa, honey, garlic, salt, and pepper in a medium bowl. Add the carrots and toss to combine. Spread in an even layer on one side of a parchment-lined rimmed baking sheet. Roast the carrots for 12 minutes.

4 Whisk together the remaining ½ tablespoon (7 ml) oil, cumin, cinnamon, and ½ teaspoon salt in a small bowl. Brush over the salmon fillets. Remove the baking sheet from the oven. Flip the carrots, and then arrange the salmon on the other side. Roast until the salmon is cooked through and easily flakes, 8 to 12 minutes depending on thickness.

5 To serve, divide the herbed millet among bowls. Top with a salmon fillet, roasted carrots, cucumber, and arugula, and drizzle with Mint Yogurt Sauce.

GLUTEN FREE | **Serves 4**

¾ cup (130 g) millet

2 cups (470 ml) water

Kosher salt and freshly ground black pepper

3 tablespoons (45 ml) avocado or extra-virgin olive oil, divided

½ cup (75 g) dried currants

¼ cup (12 g) finely chopped fresh mint

¼ cup (12 g) finely chopped fresh parsley

3 medium carrots

1½ tablespoons (9 g) harissa

1 teaspoon (6 g) honey

1 clove garlic, minced

½ teaspoon ground cumin

½ teaspoon ground cinnamon

4 (4- to 6-ounce, 115 to 168 g) salmon fillets

½ medium English cucumber, chopped

2 packed cups (40 g) arugula

1 recipe Mint Yogurt Sauce (page 27)

# Bittersweet Citrus and Salmon Power Bowls

Sweet and tangy citrus is one of the most wonderful pairings with salmon—and not just lemons, which are used so frequently, but oranges too, especially once early winter hits and those really good, perfectly ripe oranges arrive at the market. Their acidity and sweetness cut through the fattiness of salmon for a meal that feels balanced and fresh, with a subtle contrast of bitterness from a handful of jewel-toned radicchio.

Navel oranges are easy to find and work nicely with the ingredients in this bowl, but if you can find them, Cara Cara oranges or blood oranges are my preference.

**Serves 4**

Juice from 1 navel orange
3 tablespoons (45 ml) rice vinegar
2 teaspoons (10 ml) toasted sesame oil
2 teaspoons (12 g) honey
Kosher sea salt and freshly ground black pepper
1 cup (165 g) pearled farro
2½ cups (590 ml) water
4 (4- to 6-ounce, or 115 to 168 g) salmon fillets
2 tablespoons (30 ml) avocado or extra-virgin olive oil, divided
1 pound (455 g) Brussels sprouts, trimmed and halved
½ medium head radicchio, finely shredded
1 fennel bulb, trimmed and thinly sliced
2 oranges, peeled and segmented, preferably Cara Cara or blood oranges
4 scallions, green part only, thinly sliced
Toasted pistachios, chopped

1 Whisk together the orange juice, vinegar, sesame oil, honey, and a pinch of salt and pepper in a small bowl; set aside.

2 Add the farro, water, and a generous pinch of salt to a medium saucepan. Bring to a boil, then reduce the heat to medium-low, cover, and simmer until the farro is tender with a slight chew, about 30 minutes.

3 Meanwhile, arrange an oven rack 6 inches (15 cm) below the broiler, and set the oven to broil. Brush the salmon with 1 table-spoon (15 ml) of the oil and season with salt and pepper. Place the salmon skin-side down on one side of a foil-lined rimmed baking sheet. Toss the Brussels sprouts with the remaining 1 tablespoon (15 ml) oil, salt, and pepper, then spread in an even layer on the other side of the baking sheet. Broil until the salmon is cooked through and flakes easily, 6 to 8 minutes, depending on thickness.

4 To serve, divide the farro, Brussels sprouts, and radicchio among bowls. Top with salmon, fennel, orange segments, scallions, and pistachios. Whisk the dressing together once more and drizzle over the top.

# Salmon Teriyaki Bowls with Miso-Braised Kale

This Buddha bowl is just as much about the broiled salmon fillet slicked with a simple, home-made teriyaki sauce as it is about the umami-rich kale that rests next to it. In fact, the braised greens will make you fall in love with kale all over again, or win you over for the first time. They're quickly sautéed, then simmered in a miso-infused broth until tender and bursting with the kind of rich, savory flavor you don't quite expect from deep greens.

**Serves 4**

¾ cup (125 g) forbidden rice
1½ cups (355 ml) water
Kosher salt and freshly ground black pepper
¼ cup (60 ml) soy sauce
¼ cup (80 g) honey or agave
2 tablespoons (30 ml) rice vinegar
1 tablespoon (6 g) grated fresh ginger
2 cloves garlic, minced
4 (4- to 6-ounce, 115 to 168 g) salmon fillets
1¼ cups (295 ml) chicken stock
1 tablespoon (15 g) white miso paste
2 teaspoons (10 ml) mirin
1½ tablespoons (23 ml) avocado or extra-virgin olive oil
6 cups (420 g) chopped Tuscan kale
1 cup (120 g) shelled edamame
2 avocados, peeled, pitted, and thinly sliced
1 recipe Miso-Ginger Sauce (page 23)
Scallions, thinly sliced
Sesame seeds

1 Combine the rice, water, and a generous pinch of salt in a medium saucepan and bring to a boil. Reduce the heat to low, cover, and simmer, stirring occasionally, until the rice is tender, about 30 minutes.

2 Whisk together the soy sauce, honey or agave, rice vinegar, ginger, garlic, and a pinch of pepper in a shallow container large enough to hold all pieces of salmon in a single layer. Place the salmon in the dish skin-side up. Cover and refrigerate for at least 10 minutes.

3 Meanwhile, in a small bowl, whisk together the chicken stock, miso paste, and mirin until the miso paste is completely dissolved. Heat the oil in a large skillet over medium heat. Add the kale, season with salt and pepper, and cook for 2 minutes. Pour in the stock mixture and cook until the kale is tender and most of the liquid is absorbed, about 5 minutes.

4 Arrange an oven rack 6 inches (15 cm) below the broiler and set the oven to broil. Place the salmon skin-side down on a foil-lined rimmed baking sheet and discard the marinade. Broil until the salmon is cooked through and flakes easily, 6 to 8 minutes, depending on thickness.

5 To serve, divide the rice among bowls. Top with kale, salmon, edamame, and avocado. Drizzle with Miso-Ginger Sauce and sprinkle with scallions and sesame seeds.

# Tomato-Braised Cod and Barley Bowls

This bowl is my favorite example of just how incredibly easy it can be to work heart-healthy fish, like cod, into your diet. For many years I avoided cooking fish at home because I assumed it was difficult, fussy, and time-consuming. I want you to know that none of the above is true, particularly when it comes to this recipe. Cod is a mild-mannered white fish, rich in omega-3s and B12 and B6 vitamins. The thick, meaty fillets make it a great candidate for braising, where it soaks up all the aromas of the briny, herb-flecked tomato sauce.

1 Combine the barley, water, and a pinch of salt in a medium saucepan. Bring to a boil, then cover, reduce the heat to low, and simmer until tender, 30 to 40 minutes.

2 Heat the oil in a large, wide skillet over medium heat. Add the onion, garlic, and oregano. Cook, stirring occasionally, until the onion is tender, about 4 minutes. Add the crushed tomatoes, stock, capers, salt, and pepper, and stir to combine. Simmer the sauce until slightly thickened, about 4 minutes. Season the cod on both sides with salt and pepper. Add the fillets to the skillet, so they are partially submerged and spoon some of the sauce over the top. Cook until the fillets are opaque and cooked through, 6 to 8 minutes. Add the spinach, stir to combine, and cook for 1 minute longer.

3 Meanwhile, steam the broccoli.

4 To serve, divide the barley among bowls. Top with cod, broccoli, and white beans. Spoon the remaining sauce and spinach over the top.

**Serves 4**

¾ cup (125 g) pearled barley
2¼ cups (530 ml) water
Kosher salt and freshly ground black pepper
2 tablespoons (30 ml) avocado or extra-virgin olive oil
½ medium red onion, diced
2 cloves garlic, minced
2 teaspoons (2 g) dried oregano
1 (14-ounce, or 392 g) can crushed tomatoes
½ cup (120 ml) chicken stock
¼ cup (36 g) capers, drained
4 (4- to 6-ounce, 115 to 168 g) skinless cod fillets
3 packed cups (90 g) baby spinach
1 head broccoli, cut into florets
1½ cups (300 g) or 1 (14-ounce, or 392 g) can white beans, drained and rinsed

# Sesame Tuna Bowls

I felt intimidated by cooking tuna at home for much too long, but it turns out that it honestly couldn't be easier. Despite its thickness, ahi (or yellowfin) tuna only needs a quick sear on each side before it's ready to be sliced and layered in this Asian-inspired bowl. Here, the fish is first cooked with a black and white sesame crust, which adds the most irresistible delicate crunch.

**Serves 4**

4 tablespoons (60 ml) soy sauce
2 tablespoons (30 ml) rice vinegar
Juice of 1 lime
2 teaspoons (12 g) honey
1 teaspoon (5 ml) toasted sesame oil
1 tablespoon (6 g) finely grated fresh
   ginger
1 cup (165 g) forbidden rice
2 cups (470 ml) water
Kosher salt and freshly ground black
   pepper
¼ cup (36 g) white sesame seeds
2 tablespoons (18 g) black sesame
   seeds
1 pound (455 g) ahi tuna
2 tablespoons (30 ml) avocado or
   extra-virgin olive oil, divided, plus
   more for brushing the tuna
4 heads baby bok choy, trimmed and
   halved lengthwise
1 cup (120 g) shelled edamame
2 avocados, peeled, pitted, and thinly
   sliced
1 mango, peeled, pitted, and diced

1 Whisk together the soy sauce, rice vinegar, lime juice, honey, sesame oil, and ginger in a small bowl; set aside.

2 Combine the rice, water, and a generous pinch of salt in a medium saucepan, and bring to a boil. Reduce the heat to low, cover, and simmer, stirring occasionally, until the rice is tender, about 30 minutes.

3 Mix the white and black sesame seeds together in a shallow bowl or plate. Lightly brush the tuna with avocado oil and season with salt and pepper. Dredge the tuna in the sesame seeds to coat all sides. Heat 1 tablespoon (15 ml) of the oil in a skillet over medium-high heat until very hot but not smoking. Add the tuna to the pan. Sear for 2 minutes on each side. Transfer to a cutting board while you prepare the bok boy, then slice into ¼-inch (6 mm)-thick slices.

4 Heat the remaining 1 tablespoon (15 ml) oil in a skillet over medium heat. Add the bok choy and season with salt and pepper. Cook, stirring occasionally, until wilted, about 3 minutes.

5 To serve, divide the rice among bowls. Top with tuna, bok choy, edamame, avocado, and mango. Whisk the dressing again and drizzle over the bowls.

# Shrimp Summer Roll Bowls

If you enjoy Vietnamese summer rolls, this bowl will be right up your alley. It's everything you love about the handheld version, from the lightly pickled vegetables to the chewy noodles, tender shrimp, and vibrant fresh flavors down to the peanut dipping sauce. Curly carrot noodles can be made with the ever-popular spiralizer, though you can get a similar result with a julienne peeler. A couple of my local grocery stores have even started offering them pre-spiraled, in the produce section.

1 Whisk together the vinegar, lime juice, fish sauce, and sugar in a medium bowl. Add the carrot noodles and radish, and stir to coat; set aside

2 Cook the rice noodles according to the package instructions. Drain the noodles and toss with the sesame oil.

3 Heat the avocado or olive oil in a large skillet over medium-high heat until shimmering. Add the shrimp in an even layer, season with salt and pepper, and cook undisturbed until the bottoms are pink, about 1 minute. Flip the shrimp and cook, stirring occasionally, 1 to 2 minutes longer.

4 Drain the liquid from the radishes and carrots. To serve, divide the rice noodles and romaine among bowls. Top with carrot spirals, radishes, shrimp, cucumber, and avocado. Drizzle with Peanut Sauce and garnish with fresh herbs.

**Serves 4**

2 tablespoons (30 ml) rice vinegar

2 tablespoons (30 ml) freshly squeezed lime juice

1 tablespoon (15 ml) fish sauce

2 teaspoons (8 g) sugar

4 ounces (115 g) spiralized carrot noodles

1 watermelon radish, thinly sliced

4 ounces (115 g) vermicelli rice noodles

1 teaspoon (5 ml) sesame oil

1 tablespoon (15 ml) avocado or extra-virgin olive oil

1 pound (455 g) medium shrimp, peeled and deveined

Kosher salt and freshly ground black pepper

2 packed cups (110 g) chopped romaine

½ medium English cucumber, sliced

2 avocados, peeled, pitted, and thinly sliced

1 recipe Peanut Sauce (page 24)

Fresh basil or mint, for garnish (optional)

**Make It Vegetarian!** For a vegetarian-friendly bowl, skip the fish sauce and swap the shrimp for a block of cubed extra-firm tofu. There are three equally delicious approaches you can take—it all comes down to a matter of preference: Add uncooked tofu to the bowl, double the pickling liquid to marinate the tofu along with the carrots and radish, or quickly sear the tofu on the stovetop.

# Vietnamese Zucchini Noodle and Shrimp Bowls

If you've ever been curious to try your hand at Vietnamese-style cooking at home, this is a fantastic recipe to get you started. Inspired by *bun*, the Vietnamese rice noodle salad, laden with your protein of choice, a slew of vibrant and crisp fresh vegetables and herbs, and finished off with umami-rich nuoc cham, this version delivers everything you'd expect from the classic bowl, with a twist. Zucchini noodles take the place of traditional room-temperature rice noodles, and the dipping sauce serves as both a marinade for the shrimp as well as the dressing.

While I call for shrimp in the recipe, a block of tofu or even pieces of thinly sliced chicken breast both make fine substitutes. Follow the same steps for marinating and giving the protein a quick sear in a fiery hot skillet.

GLUTEN FREE | **Serves 4**

½ cup (120 ml) water
¼ cup (60 ml) freshly squeezed lime juice
3 tablespoons (45 ml) fish sauce
2 tablespoons (30 ml) rice vinegar
2 tablespoons (25 g) sugar
1 tablespoon (15 ml) garlic chili sauce
2 cloves garlic, minced
1 pound (455 g) shrimp, peeled and deveined
1 tablespoon (15 ml) avocado or extra-virgin olive oil
16 ounces (455 g) zucchini noodles
4 small carrots, peeled and shaved into ribbons
½ medium English cucumber, sliced
¼ cup (12 g) fresh mint leaves
¼ cup (12 g) fresh basil leaves
Chopped unsalted peanuts
1 lime, cut into wedges

1 Whisk the water, lime juice, fish sauce, vinegar, sugar, chili sauce, and garlic together in a small bowl.

2 Combine the shrimp with 2 to 3 tablespoons (30 to 45 ml) of the dressing in a separate bowl, toss to coat, and marinate for about 10 minutes.

3 Heat the oil in a large skillet over high heat. Add the shrimp, stirring occasionally, until pink, 2 to 3 minutes. Discard the marinade.

4 To serve, divide the zucchini noodles among bowls. Top with shrimp, carrots, cucumber, mint, basil, peanuts, and a lime wedge, and drizzle with the dressing.

# Balsamic Shrimp and Farro Bowls

Consider this bowl a glimpse into my dinner routine. You see, I'm a strong advocate for meal prep Sundays. I wasn't always, but once I saw the benefit of how a little upfront work transformed my weeknight dinner routine, I was hooked. Think of it as a gift to your future self, making weeknight dinner an affair that comes together in minutes with minimal effort. Blend together a quick, creamy sauce while a pot of farro simmers on the stovetop and a slew of vegetables roast in the oven. The shrimp sears in minutes and gets a last-minute twist with a sweet and tangy glaze.

**Serves 4**

1 cup (165 g) pearled farro
2½ cups (590 ml) water
Kosher salt and freshly ground
    pepper
2 large portobello mushroom caps,
    cut into ½-inch (1.3 cm)-thick
    slices
2 medium zucchini, sliced into ½-inch
    (1.3 cm)-thick rounds
1 red bell pepper, cored and thinly
    sliced
3 tablespoons (45 ml) avocado or
    extra-virgin olive oil, divided
2 tablespoons (30 ml) balsamic
    vinegar
1 teaspoon (6 g) honey
2 cloves garlic, minced
1 pound (455 g) shrimp, peeled and
    deveined
Micro greens
½ cup (120 ml) Avocado Sauce
    (page 17)

1 Preheat the oven to 400°F (200°C, or gas mark 6).

2 Add the farro, water, and a generous pinch of salt to a medium saucepan. Bring to a boil, then reduce the heat to low, cover, and simmer until the farro is tender with a slight chew, about 30 minutes.

3 Meanwhile, toss the mushrooms, zucchini, and bell pepper with 2 tablespoons (30 ml) of the oil, salt, and pepper. Spread in a single layer on a rimmed baking sheet. Roast until tender and lightly browned, about 20 minutes, flipping halfway through.

4 Whisk together the balsamic vinegar and honey in a small bowl; set aside. Heat the remaining 1 tablespoon (15 ml) oil in a large skillet over medium-high heat. Add the garlic and cook, stirring constantly, until fragrant, about 30 seconds. Pour in the balsamic and honey mixture, add the shrimp, and stir to coat. Cook, tossing occasionally, until opaque and cooked through, 3 to 5 minutes.

5 To serve, divide the farro among bowls. Top with roasted vegetables, shrimp, and micro greens, then drizzle with Avocado Sauce.

# Freekeh Bowls with Caramelized Onions, Warm Tomatoes, and Seared Fish

This bowl is topped with a mixture of quick-caramelized red onion, warm, jam-like tomatoes, and lots of fresh cilantro, and in my house we call this "Foster Sauce." It was the result of a game-show-esque moment when someone else did the grocery shopping and I cooked with a basket of surprise ingredients. That was over five years ago, and I've been making it ever since to spoon over all types of fish, chicken, and grain bowls. On its own, radicchio can come off as assertive and bitter, but the sweetness of the sauce and richness of the avocado keep it in check.

1 Combine the freekeh, water, and a generous pinch of salt in a medium saucepan. Bring to a boil, then reduce the heat to low and simmer for 15 minutes, stirring occasionally, until all the liquid has been absorbed and the freekeh is tender. Remove from the heat, cover with a lid, and steam for about 5 minutes.

2 Meanwhile, heat 1½ tablespoons (23 ml) of the oil in a large skillet over medium heat. Add the onion and cook, stirring occasionally, until soft, about 8 minutes. Stir in the tomatoes and garlic, and season with a pinch of salt and pepper. Cook, stirring occasionally, until the tomatoes soften and pop, about 10 minutes. Remove the skillet from the heat and stir in the cilantro.

3 Heat the remaining 1 tablespoon (15 ml) oil in a wide skillet over medium-high heat until shimmering. Pat the fish completely dry with paper towels and season on both sides with coriander, salt, and pepper. Add the fish to the skillet and sear for 2 to 3 minutes per side.

4 To serve, divide the freekeh and radicchio among bowls. Top with a fish fillet, caramelized onions and tomatoes, and avocado. Drizzle with Lemon Tahini Sauce and sprinkle with dukkah.

**Serves 4**

1 cup (165 g) cracked freekeh
2½ cups (590 ml) water
Kosher salt and freshly ground black pepper
2½ tablespoons (37 ml) avocado or extra-virgin olive oil, divided
1 medium red onion, thinly sliced
1 pint (300 g) grape tomatoes, halved
2 cloves garlic, minced
⅓ cup (5 g) chopped fresh cilantro
½ teaspoon ground coriander
4 (4- to 6-ounce, 115 to 168 g) skinless white fish fillets, like flounder, tilapia, or striped bass
½ small head radicchio, finely shredded
2 avocados, peeled, pitted, and diced
1 recipe Lemon Tahini Sauce (page 26)
Dukkah

# Superfood Salmon Bowls

There are Buddha bowls I love for their interesting ingredients and because they're downright delicious, and those I love because they're outrageously healthy and leave me feeling like a million bucks. This bowl does both—it's the whole package, with a wonderful mix of whole grains, protein, vegetables, and good fats. If you happen to score a bunch of beets with the greens still attached, save them and use them! Swap them for part or all of the kale in this recipe, or use them in another bowl, just as you would any type of dark, leafy greens. Loaded with vitamins, minerals, and antioxidants, beets, both the root and the leaves, are a nutritional powerhouse.

GLUTEN FREE

**Serves 4**

1 large sweet potato, peeled and sliced into ½-inch (1.3 cm)-thick rounds
1 tablespoon (15 ml) avocado or extra-virgin olive oil, plus more for the salmon
Kosher salt and freshly ground black pepper
4 (4- to 6-ounce, 115 to 168 g) salmon fillets
1 cup (175 g) quinoa, rinsed
2 cups (470 ml) water
2 packed cups (140 g) finely shredded Tuscan kale
2 teaspoons (10 ml) apple cider vinegar
2 large beets, peeled and shredded
2 avocados, peeled, pitted, and thinly sliced
1 cup (50 g) sunflower sprouts
Toasted walnuts
1 recipe Lemon Tahini Sauce (page 26)

1 Preheat the oven to 425°F (220°C, or gas mark 7).

2 Toss the sweet potato rounds with the oil, salt, and pepper. Arrange in a single layer on one side of a rimmed baking sheet, and roast for 10 minutes. Remove the baking sheet from the oven and flip the potatoes. Add the salmon to the baking sheet skin-side down, lightly brush with oil, and season with salt and pepper. Roast until the salmon is cooked through and easily flakes, 8 to 12 minutes depending on thickness.

3 Meanwhile, combine the quinoa, water, and a generous pinch of salt in a medium saucepan. Bring to a boil, then cover, reduce the heat to low, and simmer until tender, about 15 minutes. Remove from the heat, stir in the kale and apple cider vinegar, and cover with a lid to steam for about 5 minutes.

4 To serve, divide the quinoa and kale among bowls. Top with salmon, sweet potatoes, beets, avocado, sprouts, and walnuts. Drizzle with Lemon Tahini Sauce.

# Brown Rice Bowls with Seared Fish and Chimichurri

If you don't care for full-flavored fish like salmon or tuna but want a way to work more seafood into your diet, consider white fish, like flounder, striped bass, sole, or tilapia. They're extremely mild-mannered fish, with a plain flavor and chameleon-like ability to pick up the bold flavors they're partnered with—in this bowl, it's a bright and tangy, herb-packed Chimichurri Sauce made with cilantro and parsley.

1 Preheat the oven to 400°F (200°C, or gas mark 6).

2 Add the rice, water, and a generous pinch of salt to a medium saucepan and bring to a boil. Reduce the heat to low, cover, and cook until the rice is tender, about 40 minutes. Remove from the heat, and steam the rice with the lid on for 10 minutes.

3 Toss the carrots with 1 tablespoon (15 ml) of the oil, coriander, salt, and pepper. Spread in a single layer on a rimmed baking sheet and roast until tender, about 15 minutes.

4 Meanwhile, heat the remaining 1 tablespoon (15 ml) oil in a wide skillet over medium-high heat until shimmering. Pat the fish completely dry with paper towels and season on both sides with salt and pepper. Add the fish to the skillet and sear for 2 to 3 minutes per side.

5 To serve, divide the rice and watercress among bowls. Top with fish, roasted carrots, and edamame. Drizzle with Chimichurri Sauce and sprinkle with sliced almonds.

GLUTEN FREE

**Serves 4**

1 cup (165 g) brown rice
2 cups (470 ml) water
Kosher salt and freshly ground black pepper
8 ounces (225 g) baby carrots, halved
2 tablespoons (30 ml) avocado or extra-virgin olive oil, divided
½ teaspoon ground coriander
4 (4- to 6-ounce, 115 to 168 g) skinless white fish fillets, like flounder, tilapia, or striped bass
1 small bunch watercress, trimmed
1 cup (120 g) shelled edamame
1 recipe Chimichurri Sauce (page 19)
Sliced almonds

# Chicken and Turkey BOWLS

Ginger Peanut Soba Noodle Bowls  **78**

Green Curry Chicken and Quinoa Bowls  **79**

Quinoa and Chicken Taco Bowls with Cilantro-Lime Dressing  **80**

Dukkah-Crusted Chicken and Barley Bowls  **82**

Harissa Chicken Bowls  **83**

Warm Autumn Chicken and Wild Rice Bowls  **85**

BBQ Chicken Quinoa Bowls  **86**

Chimichurri Chicken Bowls  **87**

Peachy Basil Chicken and Rice Bowls  **88**

Spicy Thai Chicken and Brown Rice Bowls  **89**

Quick Chicken and Sweet Potato Pho Bowls  **90**

Chicken Kofta Bowls  **92**

Herbed Chicken and Root Vegetable Bowls  **93**

Smoky Lemon Brussels Sprout Bowls with Turkey Meatballs  **94**

Turkey and Cabbage Stir-Fry Bowls with Almond Butter Sauce  **95**

# Ginger Peanut Soba Noodle Bowls

I went through a phase about a year ago when I wanted nothing for lunch but instant ramen noodles. I had recently written about a hack for bringing more flavor to the noodles by simmering sliced ginger in the water, and another for stirring in a spoonful of peanut butter at the end. On their own, each was blissfully good. But together, they made my noodles irresistibly amazing and I could not stop eating them. This is a much more wholesome version loaded with juicy strips of chicken and a good mix of vegetables, no weird spice packets necessary. The starchiness of the noodles and creaminess of the peanut butter thicken the broth quite a bit, so it's not quite soupy, yet not as thick as a sauce. And there's just enough of it to gloss over each bite of vegetables, chicken, and soba noodles.

GLUTEN FREE | **Serves 4**

3 cups (705 ml) chicken stock

2 tablespoons (12 g) chopped fresh
   ginger

8 ounces (225 g) buckwheat soba
   noodles

¼ cup (65 g) smooth peanut butter

3 tablespoons (45 ml) avocado or
   extra-virgin olive oil, divided

2 boneless, skinless chicken breasts,
   pounded to ½ inch (1.3 cm) thick

Kosher salt and freshly ground black
   pepper

4 ounces (115 g) shiitake mushrooms,
   sliced

2 cloves garlic, minced

4 heads baby bok choy, trimmed and
   halved lengthwise

¼ teaspoon red pepper flakes

½ cup (55 g) shredded carrot

Sesame seeds

1 Combine the stock and ginger in a medium saucepan and simmer over low heat for 15 minutes. Add the soba noodles and cook according to the package instructions. Drain the noodles and reserve the stock. Stir the peanut butter into the remaining stock until well combined; set aside.

2 Meanwhile, heat 1 tablespoon (15 ml) of the oil in a large skillet over medium-high heat. Generously season the chicken with salt and pepper on both sides. Add the chicken to the pan and cook, undisturbed, until the bottom is well browned, about 5 minutes. Flip the chicken. Sear the other side until well browned and cooked through, another 4 to 5 minutes. Transfer the chicken to a cutting board and set aside.

3 Add another tablespoon (15 ml) of oil to the skillet, along with the mushrooms, salt, and pepper. Cook, stirring occasionally, until soft. Stir in the garlic and cook for 2 minutes longer. Transfer the mushrooms to a plate.

4 Add the remaining 1 tablespoon (15 ml) oil to the skillet along with the bok choy, salt, and red pepper flakes, and stir to coat. Cook, stirring occasionally, until wilted.

5 Slice the chicken into strips. To serve, divide the soba noodles among bowls and top with chicken, mushrooms, bok choy, and carrots. Pour the reserved peanut sauce over the top and sprinkle with sesame seeds.

# Green Curry Chicken and Quinoa Bowls

While most curries simmer all the vegetables right in the pot of sauce, this bowl is filled with a mix of cooked and raw vegetables for a variety of tender, crisp, and crunchy textures. Each bowl is finished with just enough brothy curry so that you get some with every bite. For these bowls (and all Thai curries), I prefer Thai Kitchen curry paste. It has a full, well-balanced flavor and is gluten free and shellfish free.

1 Combine the quinoa, water, and a generous pinch of salt in a medium saucepan. Bring to a boil, then cover, reduce the heat to low, and simmer until tender, about 15 minutes. Remove from the heat, keeping it covered, and steam for about 5 minutes.

2 Meanwhile, heat 1 tablespoon (14 g) of the coconut oil in a Dutch oven over medium-high heat. Generously season the chicken with salt and pepper on both sides. Add the chicken to the pan and cook, undisturbed, until the bottom is well browned, 4 to 5 minutes. Flip the chicken. Sear the other side until well browned, another 4 to 5 minutes. Transfer the chicken to a cutting board and slice once cool enough to handle.

3 Heat the remaining 1 tablespoon (14 g) coconut oil in the same pot over medium heat. Add the garlic and ginger, and cook until fragrant, about 30 seconds. Stir in the curry paste, and cook for 1 minute longer. Stir in the sweet potatoes, coconut milk, stock, and lime zest, and season with salt and pepper. Bring to a boil, then reduce the heat to low and simmer until the sweet potatoes are tender, 15 to 20 minutes. Remove from the heat and stir in the tamari.

4 To serve, divide the quinoa and chard among bowls. Top with chicken, red pepper, cabbage, and sweet potatoes. Spoon the curry sauce over the top, and garnish with fresh herbs and a squeeze of lime juice.

**Vegetable Tip!** Save the chard stems—they are totally edible! I like to toss them into the pot at the end of cooking. A few minutes is enough to mellow their bite.

GLUTEN FREE | **Serves 4**

1 cup (175 g) quinoa, rinsed
2 cups (470 ml) water
Kosher salt and freshly ground black pepper
2 tablespoons (28 g) coconut oil, divided
1 pound (455 g) boneless, skinless chicken breast, pounded to ½ inch (1.3 cm) thick
2 cloves garlic, minced
1½ tablespoons (9 g) finely chopped fresh ginger
2 tablespoons (30 g) green Thai curry paste
2 medium sweet potatoes, peeled and cut into 1-inch (2.5 cm) cubes
1 (14-ounce, or 392 g) can unsweetened coconut milk
1½ cups (355 ml) vegetable or chicken stock
1 lime, zested, then cut into wedges
2 teaspoons (10 ml) tamari
3 cups (210 g) shredded rainbow chard
1 red bell pepper, cored and thinly sliced
1 cup (70 g) shredded red cabbage
Fresh cilantro leaves
Fresh Thai basil leaves

# Quinoa and Chicken Taco Bowls with Cilantro-Lime Dressing

I have nothing against tortillas, but at some point in time I started building my tacos in a bowl, and I haven't looked back. Depending on what I have in my fridge, I make a version of this bowl weekly. It's a testament to exactly how I like my tacos: simple and straightforward with a tiny twist to keep them interesting. Here, that's a smoky and tangy dressing to perk up the shredded chicken and all the toppings.

GLUTEN FREE | **Serves 4**

¼ cup (60 ml) avocado or extra-virgin olive oil

¼ cup (60 ml) freshly squeezed lime juice

2 tablespoons (30 ml) rice vinegar

3 tablespoons (3 g) finely chopped cilantro

½ teaspoon ground cumin

Kosher salt and freshly ground black pepper

¾ cup (130 g) uncooked tricolor quinoa, rinsed

1½ cups (355 ml) water

1 pound (455 g) boneless, skinless chicken breast

2 cups (140 g) finely shredded red cabbage

1 cup (200 g) black beans, drained and rinsed

1 red or yellow bell pepper, cored and thinly sliced

1 cup (150 g) grape tomatoes, halved

1 avocado, peeled, pitted, and diced

½ medium jalapeño, seeded and sliced (optional)

1 Whisk together the oil, lime juice, vinegar, cilantro, cumin, salt, and pepper in a small bowl until emulsified. Set aside.

2 Combine the quinoa, water, and a generous pinch of salt in a medium saucepan. Bring to a boil, then cover, reduce the heat to low, and simmer until tender, about 15 minutes. Remove from the heat, and steam with the lid on for about 5 minutes.

3 Meanwhile, arrange the chicken in a single layer in a large sauce-pan. Add cold water to cover the chicken by about an inch (2.5 cm). Bring the water to a boil over medium-high heat. Reduce the heat to low and simmer until the chicken is cooked through, 10 to 14 minutes, depending on thickness. Transfer the chicken to a cutting board or large plate and shred with two forks.

4 To serve, divide the quinoa among bowls. Top with shredded chicken, cabbage, black beans, bell pepper, tomatoes, avocado, and jalapeño (if using). Drizzle with the cilantro-lime dressing.

**Cooking Tip!** One of the reasons I love poaching is because it's incredibly easy to infuse the chicken with so much flavor. Cilantro stems, cumin seeds, a couple cloves of smashed garlic, even a peel of orange zest all work nicely here.

# Dukkah-Crusted Chicken and Barley Bowls

If you add just one more item to your spice cabinet, make it dukkah. It's a lovely aromatic Egyptian spice blend made from a mixture of crushed nuts and seeds—typically coriander, cumin, fennel, sesame seeds, and hazelnuts or pistachios. Here, it blankets the chicken breast for a fragrant, savory crust with a little bit of crunch.

**Serves 4**

¾ cup (125 g) pearled barley
2¼ cups (530 ml) water
Kosher salt and freshly ground black pepper
3 medium fennel bulbs, trimmed and cut into big chunks
2 tablespoons (30 ml) avocado or extra-virgin olive oil, divided, plus more for the chicken
¼ cup (24 g) dukkah
1 pound (455 g) boneless, skinless chicken breast
2 packed cups (40 g) arugula
1 pink grapefruit, peeled and segmented
2 avocados, peeled, pitted, and diced
1 recipe Lemon Tahini Sauce (page 26)
Fennel fronds, for garnish

1 Preheat the oven to 400°F (200°C, or gas mark 6).

2 Combine the barley, water, and a generous pinch of salt in a medium saucepan. Bring to a boil, then cover, reduce the heat to low, and simmer until tender, 30 to 40 minutes.

3 Toss the fennel with 1 tablespoon (15 ml) of the oil, salt, and pepper. Arrange in a single layer on one side of a rimmed baking sheet. Roast for 15 minutes, while you prepare the chicken.

4 Meanwhile, place the dukkah in a shallow bowl or on a plate. Lightly brush the chicken with oil and coat with dukkah on all sides. Heat the remaining 1 tablespoon (15 ml) oil in a large skillet over medium-high heat. Add the chicken and sear until the dukkah is lightly browned, 3 to 4 minutes per side. Remove the baking sheet from the oven, stir the fennel, and place the chicken on the other side. Continue cooking until the chicken is cooked through, 6 to 10 minutes longer, depending on thickness. Rest the chicken for a few minutes, then slice.

5 To serve, divide the barley and arugula among bowls. Top with sliced chicken, fennel, grapefruit segments, and avocado. Drizzle with Lemon Tahini Sauce and garnish with fennel fronds and an extra sprinkle of dukkah.

> **More Ways to Use Dukkah**
> Dukkah is remarkably versatile. Beyond chicken, it can be used to coat everything from other meats to fish, tofu, and tempeh. Sprinkle it over a pan of roasted vegetables or mix it into greens sautéed on the stovetop.

# Harissa Chicken Bowls

The most treasured cookbook (a binder, really) in our kitchen was put together by my late mother-in-law, Kate, and gifted to my husband long before we met. It's filled with her handwritten recipes and notes, many family favorites, and, most notably, some well-worn pages with mysterious food splatters that tell me they've been well loved and cooked often. In it she shares a recipe for her version of harissa chicken that I instantly fell in love with and have now made more times than I can remember. Her recipe also serves as the inspiration for this bowl.

Just as Kate intends in her recipe, there's just enough spicy harissa—coated on the chicken and stirred into the freekeh—to keep you on your toes without overwhelming your palate. It's balanced with a light, cooling Mint Feta Sauce, seared jammy tomatoes, greens, and chickpeas.

1 Preheat the oven to 400°F (200°C, or gas mark 6).

2 Add the chicken to a large bowl along with the cumin, coriander, cardamom, salt, and pepper. Toss until the chicken is well coated; set aside while you prep the vegetables and freekeh.

3 Toss the zucchini with 1 tablespoon (15 ml) of the oil, salt, and pepper. Spread in a single layer on a rimmed baking sheet. Roast for 20 minutes, flipping halfway through.

4 Meanwhile, combine the freekeh, water, and a generous pinch of salt in a medium saucepan. Bring to a boil, then reduce the heat to low, cover, and simmer for 15 minutes, stirring occasionally, until all the liquid has been absorbed and the freekeh is tender. Remove from the heat and stir in 1 tablespoon (15 ml) of oil and 1 teaspoon (2 g) of the harissa.

5 Heat the remaining 1 tablespoon (15 ml) oil in a large skillet over high heat until very hot but not smoking. Add the chicken and sear on all sides, 1 to 2 minutes per side. Stir in the tomatoes and cook just until they begin to pop, about 2 minutes. Add the remaining 1 table-spoon (6 g) harissa and chicken stock, and stir to combine. Bring to a boil, then reduce the heat to low, and simmer for 3 minutes.

6 To serve, divide the freekeh and Swiss chard among bowls. Top with chicken and tomatoes, roasted zucchini, fennel, and chickpeas. Drizzle with Creamy Mint Feta Sauce.

**Serves 4**

1 pound (455 g) boneless, skinless chicken breast, cut into 1-inch (2.5 cm) cubes
1 teaspoon (2 g) ground cumin
1 teaspoon (2 g) ground coriander
½ teaspoon ground cardamom
Kosher salt and freshly ground black pepper
2 medium zucchini, sliced into ½-inch (1.3 cm)-thick rounds
3 tablespoons (45 ml) avocado or extra-virgin olive oil, divided
¾ cup (125 g) cracked freekeh
2 cups (470 ml) water
1 tablespoon (6 g) plus 1 teaspoon (2 g) harissa, divided
2 cups (300 g) cherry tomatoes
½ cup (120 ml) chicken stock
2 cups (140 g) chopped Swiss chard
1 medium bulb fennel, trimmed and thinly sliced
1½ cups (300 g) or 1 (15-ounce, or 420 g) can chickpeas, drained and rinsed
1 recipe Creamy Mint Feta Sauce (variation page 20)

# Warm Autumn Chicken and Wild Rice Bowls

Once the cool chill of early autumn enters the air, I feel a distinct shift in the foods I crave. Big bowls of fresh salads and light, herb-filled meals give way to smoky roasted vegetables, warm spices, and hearty grains. Here is a wholesome, autumn-inspired meal that captures all of that in one loaded bowl, packed with chewy wild rice, juicy, ginger-infused shredded chicken, crispy Brussels sprouts, and roasted winter squash. A handful of spicy arugula keeps the bowl feeling fresh, while a sprinkle of toasted pumpkin seeds adds a welcome crunch.

In addition to the mingling of warm flavors that fill this bowl, its make-ahead potential is not to be missed. Because of wild rice's long cook time, I recommend making it a day or two in advance. While you're at it, pop the vegetables in the oven and poach the chicken at the same time, then store everything in the fridge until it's time to eat.

1 Preheat the oven to 425°F (220°C, or gas mark 7).

2 Combine the rice, water, and a generous pinch of salt in a medium saucepan. Bring to a boil. Lower the heat to maintain a steady simmer, cover, and cook until the grains are tender and some have burst open, 45 to 50 minutes. Drain excess liquid, if necessary. Meanwhile, prepare the roasted vegetables and chicken.

3 Slice the squash in half lengthwise. Scoop out the seeds. Slice crosswise into ½-inch (1.3 cm)-thick crescents. Toss the squash and Brussels sprouts with the oil, and season with salt and pepper. Arrange in a single layer on a rimmed baking sheet. Roast until tender, 20 to 25 minutes, stirring the Brussels sprouts and flipping the squash halfway through.

4 Meanwhile, add the chicken and ginger to a large saucepan in a single layer, and cover with cool water by 2 inches (5 cm). Bring to a boil, then reduce the heat to low, and simmer until the chicken is cooked through, 10 to 12 minutes, depending on thickness. Transfer the chicken to a cutting board or large plate and use two forks to shred the meat.

5 To serve, divide the rice among bowls. Top with shredded chicken, squash, Brussels sprouts, and arugula. Drizzle with Spicy Maple Tahini Sauce and garnish with pumpkin seeds and pomegranate arils.

GLUTEN FREE | **Serves 4**

¾ cup (125 g) wild rice, rinsed
3 cups (705 ml) water
Kosher salt and freshly ground black pepper
2 small delicata squash
1 pound (455 g) Brussels sprouts, halved
2 tablespoons (30 ml) avocado or extra-virgin olive oil
1 pound (455 g) boneless, skinless chicken breast
2-inch (5 cm) piece ginger, thinly sliced
2 cups (40 g) arugula
1 recipe Spicy Maple Tahini Sauce (page 26)
Toasted pumpkin seeds
Pomegranate arils

# BBQ Chicken Quinoa Bowls

I have strong feelings about poaching chicken breast. Namely, that this cooking technique is wildly underrated and not used nearly enough. Except, perhaps, in my home, where at some point along the way it became a regular part of my meal prep routine. Poaching requires such little time and effort, yet rewards you with reliably juicy meat that I love pulling into fringy shreds. While it feels like there are a million and one ways to turn shredded chicken into a meal, this bowl has secured the top spot as my favorite. It's packed with just the right balance of bright, earthy, and tangy flavors, and topped with a light yogurt sauce that's mixed with herbs to mimic ranch dressing.

When it comes to the BBQ sauce, any variety will work. I aspire to make my own, but until that time comes I stick with brands made with whole food ingredients and no, or very little, added sugar.

GLUTEN FREE | **Serves 4**

3 medium sweet potatoes, peeled and sliced into ½-inch (1.3 cm)-thick rounds
1 tablespoon (15 ml) avocado or extra-virgin olive oil
Kosher salt and freshly ground black pepper
1 pound (455 g) boneless, skinless chicken breast
½ cup (120 ml) BBQ sauce, more as needed
¾ cup (130 g) quinoa, rinsed
1½ cups (355 ml) water
2 packed cups (60 g) baby spinach
2 avocados, peeled, pitted, and diced
Red cabbage sauerkraut
½ cup (120 ml) Yogurt Ranch Sauce (page 27)

1 Preheat the oven to 425°F (220°C, or gas mark 7).

2 Toss the sweet potato slices with the oil and season with salt and pepper. Arrange in a single layer on a rimmed baking sheet. Roast for 20 minutes, flipping the potatoes halfway through.

3 Add the chicken to a large saucepan in a single layer and cover by about 2 inches (5 cm) with cool water. Bring to a boil, then reduce the heat to low, and simmer until the chicken is cooked through, 10 to 14 minutes, depending on thickness.

4 Transfer the chicken to a cutting board or large plate and use two forks to shred the meat. Discard the water and rinse the pan. Return the meat to the pan with the BBQ sauce and stir together.

5 Combine the quinoa, water, and a generous pinch of salt in a medium saucepan. Bring to a boil, then cover, reduce the heat to low, and simmer until tender, about 15 minutes. Remove from the heat, and steam with the lid on for about 5 minutes.

6 To serve, divide the quinoa and spinach among bowls. Top with sweet potatoes, shredded chicken, avocado, and sauerkraut, then drizzle with Yogurt Ranch Sauce.

# Chimichurri Chicken Bowls

Herby, bold Chimichurri Sauce is my secret weapon for perking up basic chicken and rice Buddha bowls. It's a piquant sauce packed with a bundle of herbs and a pop of tangy, bright flavor. To really get the most out of it, I use it as both a marinade for the chicken and the sauce for the finished bowl. It's worth planning ahead when making this bowl, so you can allow the chicken ample time to marinate. I recommend at least an hour, though if you have time for the chicken to marinate all day or even overnight, that's even better.

1 Preheat the oven to 425°F (220°C, or gas mark 7).

2 Add the chicken to a large bowl along with 2 tablespoons (30 ml) of the Chimichurri Sauce. Toss so the chicken is evenly coated. Cover and marinate in the refrigerator for at least 1 hour.

3 Add the rice, water, and a generous pinch of salt to a medium saucepan, and bring to a boil. Reduce the heat to low, cover, and cook until the rice is tender, about 40 minutes. Remove from the heat, and steam the rice with the lid on for 10 minutes.

4 Toss the peppers with the oil, salt, and pepper, and spread in an even layer on one side of a rimmed baking sheet. Remove the chicken thighs from the marinade and add to the other side of the baking sheet. Roast for 10 minutes, then flip the peppers. Continue roasting until the chicken is cooked through and the peppers are lightly browned, 10 to 15 minutes longer.

5 To serve, divide the rice among bowls. Top with chicken, roasted peppers, red cabbage, and avocado. Spoon the remaining Chimichurri Sauce over the top and sprinkle with toasted pumpkin seeds.

GLUTEN FREE | **Serves 4**

4 boneless, skinless chicken thighs (about 1 pound, or 455 g)
1 recipe Chimichurri Sauce (page 19)
1 cup (165 g) brown rice
2 cups (470 ml) water
Kosher salt and freshly ground black pepper
8 piquillo peppers
1 tablespoon (15 ml) avocado or extra-virgin olive oil
1½ cups (105 g) finely shredded red cabbage
2 avocados, peeled, pitted, and thinly sliced
Toasted pumpkin seeds

# Peachy Basil Chicken and Rice Bowls

I could eat chicken and rice bowls every single week and never get tired of them. My trick is adding a couple of fresh, flavorful, and slightly unexpected ingredients to keep the bowls interesting. In this case, it's slices of juicy, ripe peach and a generous handful of spicy basil. They partner together incredibly well and offer mild-mannered chicken breast a super fresh and slightly sweet twist.

I prefer using fresh peaches whenever possible, but when they're out of season, frozen peaches make a fine substitute. Add about six ounces straight from the freezer into the skillet with the chicken and basil, and they'll warm and soften nicely against the heat of the pan.

**Serves 4**

1 cup (165 g) jasmine rice, rinsed
2 cups (470 ml) water
Kosher salt and freshly ground black
    pepper
1 pound (455 g) boneless, skinless
    chicken breast, cut into 1½-inch
    (3.8 cm) cubes
2 tablespoons (16 g) all-purpose flour
2 tablespoons (30 ml) avocado or
    extra-virgin olive oil, divided
1 tablespoon (14 g) ghee or unsalted
    butter
¼ cup (12 g) chopped fresh basil
1 peach, pitted and thinly sliced
6 packed cups (180 g) baby spinach
2 cloves garlic, minced
½ medium English cucumber, sliced
1 small fennel bulb, trimmed and
    thinly sliced
1 recipe Basil Goat Cheese Sauce,
    (variation page 22)

1 Add the rice, water, and a generous pinch of salt to a medium saucepan, and bring to a boil. Reduce the heat, cover, and cook until the rice is tender, about 15 minutes. Remove from the heat, and steam the rice with the lid on for 10 minutes.

2 Pat the chicken dry with paper towels. Place in a large bowl with the flour, salt, and pepper, and toss to evenly coat the chicken. Heat 1 tablespoon (15 ml) of the oil in a large, wide skillet over high heat until very hot but not yet smoking. Add the chicken to the pan in a single layer and cook, turning occasionally, until golden brown on all sides, about 5 minutes total. Add the ghee, basil, and sliced peach to the skillet and cook for 1 minute longer, stirring to coat the chicken.

3 Meanwhile, in a separate skillet, heat the remaining 1 tablespoon (15 ml) oil over medium heat. Add the spinach, garlic, and a pinch of salt. Cook, tossing regularly, until wilted, 2 to 3 minutes.

4 To serve, divide the rice among bowls. Top with chicken and peaches, spinach, cucumber, and fennel, and then drizzle with Basil Goat Cheese Sauce.

# Spicy Thai Chicken and Brown Rice Bowls

I first picked up a pack of ground chicken a few years ago on a whim, and boy did I wish I'd been cooking with it all along. It's a leaner alternative to beef, lamb, and pork, with a mild flavor that's all too willing to partner with any herb, sauce, or vegetable. These days, it's my top pick for bulking up rice bowls for dinner. If you regularly cook with ground turkey, ground chicken is a nice way to change things up. When it's available or I can get the meat freshly ground at the butcher, I opt for a mix of light and dark meat. The light breast meat keeps the mixture lean, while the dark leg meat adds a boost of fat and flavor. For this bowl, the ground chicken is quickly browned and broken into crumbles on the stovetop, then mixed with a Thai red curry peanut sauce.

1 Add the rice, water, and a generous pinch of salt to a medium saucepan, and bring to a boil. Reduce the heat to low, cover, and cook until the rice is tender, about 40 minutes. Remove from the heat, and steam the rice with the lid on for 10 minutes.

2 Heat 1 tablespoon (14 g) of the coconut oil in a large skillet over medium-high heat. Add the bell pepper, season with a pinch of salt and pepper, and cook, tossing occasionally, until just soft, about 4 minutes. Transfer to a plate.

3 Heat the remaining 1 tablespoon (14 g) coconut oil in the skillet. Add the chicken, garlic, and cayenne, season with salt and pepper, and cook, breaking up the meat with a wooden spoon, until browned and cooked through, 6 to 8 minutes. Stir in half of the scallions and 2 tablespoons (30 ml) of the Curried Peanut Sauce, and cook for 1 minute longer.

4 To serve, divide the cabbage and carrots among bowls. Top with brown rice, ground chicken, bell pepper, and fresh basil. Drizzle with the remaining Curried Peanut Sauce and sprinkle with the remaining scallions and peanuts.

GLUTEN FREE | **Serves 4**

1 cup (165 g) brown rice
2 cups (470 ml) water
Kosher salt and freshly ground black pepper
2 tablespoons (28 g) coconut oil, divided
1 red bell pepper, cored and thinly sliced
1 pound (455 g) ground chicken
2 cloves garlic, minced
½ teaspoon cayenne pepper
2 scallions, thinly sliced, divided
¾ cup (180 ml) Curried Peanut Sauce (page 24), divided
2 cups (140 g) finely shredded red cabbage
1 cup (110 g) shredded carrot
Chopped fresh Thai basil leaves
Chopped peanuts

# Quick Chicken and Sweet Potato Pho Bowls

While traveling through Vietnam, I happily adopted in no time the ritual of slurping down hot bowls of pho for breakfast every day. It was far outside of my regular routine, but also far too calming and nourishing to pass up. I clung to those morning memories when I got home, and created my own weeknight-friendly version of noodle soup bowls with dinner in mind. Here, traditional rice noodles are swapped for spiraled sweet potato noodles, and the chicken is poached in a simmering broth perfumed with ginger and spices for extra flavor.

**GLUTEN FREE | Serves 4**

1 medium onion, chopped

2-inch (5 cm) piece fresh ginger, peeled and halved

1 tablespoon (15 ml) avocado or extra-virgin olive oil

4 ounces (115 g) shiitake mushrooms, thinly sliced

4 chicken cutlets

4 cups (940 ml) chicken broth

2 tablespoons (30 ml) fish sauce

1 cinnamon stick

2 star anise

3 whole cloves

Kosher salt and freshly ground black pepper

16 ounces (455 g) sweet potato noodles

1 cup (75 g) snap peas, halved

4 radishes, thinly sliced

2 scallions, thinly sliced

Bean sprouts

Sliced jalapeño

Cilantro

Lime wedges

1 Arrange an oven rack about 6 inches (15 cm) below the broiler, and set the oven to broil. Place the onion and ginger on a rimmed baking sheet and broil until lightly charred, about 5 minutes.

2 Heat the oil in a skillet over medium-high heat. Sauté the mushrooms until tender and lightly seared, about 5 minutes; set aside.

3 Add the onion, ginger, chicken, broth, fish sauce, cinnamon, star anise, and cloves to a large saucepan. Bring to a boil, then reduce the heat and simmer until the chicken is cooked through, about 8 minutes. Transfer the chicken to a cutting board, cool slightly, and slice.

4 Remove the ginger, cinnamon, star anise, and cloves from the saucepan. Return to the heat, and season the broth with salt and pepper to taste. Add the sweet potato noodles and cook until just tender, about 3 minutes.

5 To serve, divide the noodles among bowls. Top with sliced chicken, mushrooms, snap peas, radish, scallions, bean sprouts, jalapeño, and cilantro. Pour the broth over the top and garnish with a lime wedge.

# Chicken Kofta Bowls

This bowl celebrates the versatility of meatballs. Eaten widely across the Middle East and parts of Asia, kofta is a type of meatball or meat patty made with ground meat and a mix of fresh herbs and spices that vary based on origin. This version, made with ground chicken, is bursting with freshness from parsley and mint.

**Serves 4**

1 small bunch beets, greens separated
2 tablespoons (30 ml) avocado or
    extra-virgin olive oil, divided
Kosher salt and freshly ground black
    pepper
1 pound (455 g) ground chicken
½ cup (24 g) finely chopped fresh
    parsley
¼ cup (12 g) finely chopped fresh
    mint
¼ cup (40 g) finely diced red onion
3 cloves garlic, minced, divided
1 teaspoon (2 g) ground cumin
1 teaspoon (2 g) ground coriander
¾ cup (125 g) bulgur
1½ cups (355 ml) water
1 teaspoon (5 ml) apple cider vinegar
1 recipe Harissa Yogurt Sauce
    (page 27)
Toasted pine nuts

**Ingredient Tip** | If you have a hard time finding beets with the greens still attached, not to worry. Simply swap in another type of dark greens, like turnip greens, mustard greens, collards, or kale.

1 Preheat the oven to 425°F (220°C, or gas mark 7).

2 Chop the greens and stems (4 to 6 cups, or 280 to 420 g total) and set aside, then peel and cut the beetroot into 1-inch (2.5 cm) cubes. Toss with 1 tablespoon (15 ml) of the oil, season with salt and pepper, and arrange in a single layer on a rimmed baking sheet. Roast until tender, about 30 minutes, stirring halfway through.

3 Meanwhile, combine the chicken, herbs, onion, 2 cloves of the garlic, cumin, coriander, ½ teaspoon of salt, and ¼ teaspoon of freshly ground pepper in a large bowl. Mix until evenly combined. Scoop out about 2 tablespoons (30 g) of the mixture and roll between the palms of your hands into a 2- to 3-inch (5 to 7.5 cm) oval with tapered ends. Arrange about 1 inch (2.5 cm) apart on a parchment-lined rimmed baking sheet. Roast until the meatballs are cooked through, about 15 minutes.

4 Combine the bulgur, water, and a generous pinch of salt in a medium saucepan. Bring to a boil, then cover, reduce the heat to low, and simmer until tender, 10 to 15 minutes.

5 Meanwhile, heat the remaining 1 tablespoon (15 ml) oil in a large skillet over medium heat. Add the beet greens, remaining 1 clove garlic, and a pinch of salt and pepper. Cook, tossing occasionally, until wilted, about 4 minutes. Remove from the heat and stir in the apple cider vinegar.

6 To serve, divide the bulgur among bowls. Top with chicken kofta, roasted beetroot, and beet greens. Drizzle with Harissa Yogurt Sauce and sprinkle with pine nuts.

# Herbed Chicken and Root Vegetable Bowls

Chicken thighs are one of my absolute favorite cuts of meat to cook. Unlike the lean, mild-mannered chicken breast, thighs, considered the "dark meat" of the bird, are a fattier cut, with a rich, full-flavored taste that are less prone to drying out. As an added bonus, they're also wonderfully inexpensive. Here, they're blanketed with a simple, tangy, herb-flecked coating and roasted alongside sweet, earthy root vegetables. When I have the forethought to plan ahead, I like to let the chicken thighs marinate for as much extra time as I have available so they can soak up as much flavor as possible.

1 Preheat the oven to 425°F (220°C, or gas mark 7).

2 Combine the wild rice, water, and a generous pinch of salt in a medium saucepan. Bring to a boil. Lower the heat to maintain a steady simmer, cover, and cook for 10 minutes. Stir in the brown rice and cook until the grains are tender and the water is absorbed, 35 to 45 minutes longer.

3 Toss the sweet potato with 1 tablespoon (15 ml) of the oil, salt, and pepper. Spread in a single layer on a rimmed baking sheet. Toss the carrots and parsnips with 1 tablespoon (15 ml) of oil, paprika, salt, and pepper and spread in a single layer on one side of a separate rimmed baking sheet.

4 Whisk together the remaining 2 tablespoons (30 ml) oil, vinegar, garlic, thyme, rosemary, red pepper flakes (if using), salt, and pepper in a large bowl. Add the chicken thighs and toss to coat. Add to the baking sheet with the carrots and parsnips. Roast both pans until the chicken is cooked through and the vegetables are tender, 20 to 25 minutes.

5 To serve, divide the rice among bowls. Top with chicken, sweet potato, carrots, parsnips, shredded beets, and Tangy Tahini Sauce.

GLUTEN FREE | **Serves 4**

½ cup (82 g) wild rice, rinsed
3 cups (705 ml) water
Kosher salt and freshly ground black pepper
½ cup (82 g) brown rice
1 large sweet potato, peeled and cut into ½-inch (1.3 cm)-thick rounds
4 tablespoons (60 ml) avocado or extra-virgin olive oil, divided
2 medium carrots, peeled and cut into ½-inch (1.3 cm)-thick slices
2 medium parsnips, peeled and cut into ½-inch (1.3 cm)-thick slices
2 teaspoons (4 g) paprika
1 tablespoon (15 ml) apple cider vinegar
2 cloves garlic, minced
1 teaspoon dried thyme
1 teaspoon dried rosemary
¼ teaspoon red pepper flakes (optional)
4 boneless, skinless chicken thighs (about 1 pound, or 455 g)
2 medium beets, peeled and shredded
1 recipe Tangy Tahini Sauce (page 26)

# Smoky Lemon Brussels Sprout Bowls with Turkey Meatballs

Meatballs, particularly those made with lean turkey, have become one of my favorite ways to round out Buddha bowls with a boost of protein. Their mild flavor means they're easy to pair with just about any topping, and this oven-baked version cooks up tender and juicy. Smoked paprika and fresh lemon juice might seem like an unlikely match for Brussels sprouts, but they add a warm, bright twist that really works well.

GLUTEN FREE | **Serves 4**

¾ cup (125 g) wild rice, rinsed

3 cups (705 ml) water

Kosher salt and freshly ground black pepper

1 pound (455 g) ground turkey

¼ cup (40 g) grated red onion

3 cloves garlic, minced, divided

2 tablespoons (6 g) finely chopped fresh parsley

6 ounces (168 g) cremini mushrooms, halved

2 tablespoons (30 ml) avocado or extra-virgin olive oil, divided

¾ pound (340 g) Brussels sprouts, trimmed and finely shredded

1 teaspoon (2 g) smoked paprika

Zest and juice of ½ lemon

1 large beet, peeled and thinly sliced

1 recipe Light and Creamy Goat Cheese Sauce (page 22)

1 Preheat the oven to 425°F (220°C, or gas mark 7).

2 Combine the rice, water, and a generous pinch of salt in a medium saucepan. Bring to a boil. Lower the heat to maintain a steady simmer, cover, and cook until the grains are tender and some have burst open, 45 to 50 minutes. Drain excess liquid, if necessary. Meanwhile, prepare the roasted vegetables and turkey.

3 Add the turkey, onion, 2 cloves of the garlic, parsley, and ½ teaspoon of salt to a large bowl. Mix with your hands until the ingredients are evenly combined. Do not overwork the meat. Scoop out about 1½ tablespoons (23 g) of the mixture and roll into a ball between the palms of your hands. Arrange about 1 inch (2.5 cm) apart on one side of a parchment-lined rimmed baking sheet.

4 Toss the mushrooms with 1 tablespoon (15 ml) of the oil, salt, and pepper. Spread on the other side of the baking sheet. Roast until the meatballs are cooked through and the mushrooms are browned, about 15 minutes.

5 Heat the remaining 1 tablespoon (15 ml) oil in a large skillet over medium heat. Add the Brussels sprouts, remaining 1 clove garlic, paprika, lemon zest, salt, and pepper. Stir to coat with the oil, and cook until the Brussels sprouts are crisp and tender, about 5 minutes. Remove from the heat and stir in the lemon juice.

6 To serve, divide the wild rice among bowls. Top with meatballs, mushrooms, Brussels sprouts, and beets. Drizzle with Light and Creamy Goat Cheese Sauce.

# Turkey and Cabbage Stir-Fry Bowls with Almond Butter Sauce

I have a long history of cobbling together meals by pulling odds and ends from the fridge and pantry, adding a little of this and a little of that. Such is how one of my favorite stir-fries, and the inspiration for this bowl, came to be. I've now made this more times than I can remember and can confidently say it is even better than the original version.

1 Preheat the oven to 400°F (200°C, or gas mark 6).

2 Add the almond butter, ¼ cup (60 ml) of the coconut aminos, lime juice, red pepper flakes, salt, and pepper to a small bowl. Stir well until combined.

3 Cook the rice noodles according to the package instructions. Drain, rinse well, and set aside.

4 Toss the broccolini with 1 tablespoon (14 g) of the coconut oil and season with salt and pepper. Arrange in a single layer on a rimmed baking sheet. Roast for 20 minutes, stirring once halfway through.

5 Heat 1 tablespoon (14 g) of coconut oil in a large skillet over medium-high heat. Add the turkey and season with salt and pepper. Cook, breaking up the meat with a wooden spoon, until it starts to brown. Add 2 cloves of the garlic and the ginger, and continue cooking until the meat is browned and cooked through. Stir in 2 tablespoons (30 ml) of the almond butter sauce.

6 Heat the remaining 1 tablespoon (14 g) coconut oil in a separate skillet. Add the cabbage and the remaining 1 clove garlic, season with salt and pepper, and cook, tossing occasionally, until soft, 3 to 5 minutes. Stir in the remaining 1 tablespoon (15 ml) coconut aminos and cook until reduced.

7 To serve, divide the rice noodles among bowls. Top with turkey, cabbage, broccolini, and zucchini. Drizzle with the remaining almond butter sauce and sprinkle with sesame seeds.

GLUTEN FREE | **Serves 4**

½ cup (130 g) creamy almond butter
¼ cup (60 ml) plus 1 tablespoon (15 ml) coconut aminos, divided
Juice from ½ lime
¼ teaspoon red pepper flakes
Kosher salt and freshly ground pepper
6 ounces (168 g) dried rice noodles
2 bunches broccolini
3 tablespoons (42 g) coconut oil, divided
1 pound (455 g) ground turkey
3 cloves garlic, minced, divided
2 tablespoons (12 g) chopped fresh ginger
6 cups (420 g) shredded red cabbage
2 medium zucchini, sliced
Sesame seeds

# Beef and Lamb
# BOWLS

Steak Fajita Spaghetti Squash Bowls **98**

Summertime Green Goddess Steak Bowls **99**

Beef and Broccoli Bowls **100**

Korean-Style Beef Bowls with Zucchini Noodles **102**

Miso Noodle Bowls with Stir-Fried Beef **103**

Ginger Beef Bowls **105**

Winter Chili Bowls with Beef, Beans, and Greens **106**

Greek Power Bowls **107**

Stuffed Eggplant Bowls with Spiced Lamb **108**

Lamb Kebab Bowls **109**

Lamb Meatball Bowls with Sweet Potato Noodles
and Green Tahini **110**

Lentil Quinoa Bowls with Harissa Lamb Meatballs **111**

Cauliflower Tabbouleh Bowls with Lamb Meatballs **112**

Lamb and Roasted Cauliflower Taco Bowls with
Chimichurri **113**

# Steak Fajita Spaghetti Squash Bowls

Often the best inspiration for creating a Buddha bowl comes from the everyday meals and recipes you're already familiar with. Case in point: steak fajitas. This version is inspired by my favorite fajitas and skips the tortillas in favor of a whole lot more veggies. Thin slices of juicy, cumin-rubbed steak are partnered with lightly charred peppers and onions, as well as cabbage and tomatoes for some extra crunch, then layered over a bowl of warm spaghetti squash strands. And, of course, no fajitas would be complete without a generous scoop of guac and Greek yogurt.

GLUTEN FREE | **Serves 4**

1 medium spaghetti squash (about 4 pounds, or 1820 g)
1 pound (455 g) flank steak
½ teaspoon ground cumin
½ teaspoon sweet paprika
Kosher salt and freshly ground black pepper
2 tablespoons (30 ml) avocado or extra-virgin olive oil, divided
1 large sweet yellow onion, thinly sliced
2 bell peppers, cored and thinly sliced
2 cups (140 g) shredded red cabbage
1½ cups (225 g) grape tomatoes, halved
1½ cups (300 g) or 1 (15-ounce, or 420 g) can black beans, drained and rinsed
Greek yogurt
¾ cup (180 ml) Avocado Sauce (page 17)

1 Preheat the oven to 400°F (200°C, or gas mark 6).

2 Cut the squash in half lengthwise, from stem to tail, then scoop out and discard the seeds. Place the squash cut-side down in a baking dish, and add about an inch (2.5 cm) of water at the bottom. Roast until the squash is tender and the strands separate easily, 40 to 50 minutes.

3 Use a fork to pull the squash flesh into strands and away from the peel. Divide among bowls.

4 Meanwhile, season the steak with the cumin, paprika, salt, and pepper on both sides. Heat ½ tablespoon (7 ml) of the oil in a cast-iron skillet over medium-high heat until very hot but not smoking. Sear the steak for 5 minutes on each side. Transfer to a cutting board.

5 Reduce the heat to medium and add the remaining 1½ tablespoons (23 ml) oil to the skillet. Add the onion, peppers, salt, and pepper, and cook, stirring occasionally, until soft and lightly browned around the edges, about 8 minutes.

6 Slice the steak against the grain into thin slices. To serve, add the cabbage to the bowls with the spaghetti squash. Top with steak, onions and peppers, tomatoes, black beans, Greek yogurt, and Avocado Sauce.

# Summertime Green Goddess Steak Bowls

When I have a hankering for steak, which I make a point to eat in moderation just once or twice a month, I pick up flank steak more than any other cut. It's a budget-friendly piece of meat, with just enough fat to give it tons of flavor, without imparting a tough, chewy bite. And when it comes to cooking, it doesn't need much more than a good sear in a screaming-hot skillet before it's ready to get topped on this bowl filled with summer fresh veggies.

1 Preheat the oven to 400°F (200°C, or gas mark 6).

2 Combine the quinoa, water, and a generous pinch of salt in a medium saucepan. Bring to a boil, then reduce the heat to a simmer and cook, uncovered, until tender, about 15 minutes. Remove from the heat, cover with a lid, and steam for about 5 minutes.

3 Meanwhile, toss the squash and zucchini with 1 tablespoon (15 ml) of the oil, salt, and pepper, then arrange in a single layer on a rimmed baking sheet. Roast until tender and lightly browned, about 15 minutes, flipping once halfway through.

4 Heat the remaining 1 tablespoon (15 ml) oil in a cast-iron skillet over medium-high heat until very hot but not smoking. Pat the steak dry with a paper towel, and season generously on both sides with salt and pepper. Sear the steak for 5 minutes on each side. Transfer to a cutting board.

5 Slice the steak against the grain into thin slices. To serve, divide the arugula among bowls. Top with roasted squash and zucchini, quinoa, steak, tomatoes, and corn, then drizzle with Avocado Green Goddess Dressing.

GLUTEN FREE | **Serves 4**

¾ cup (130 g) quinoa, rinsed
1½ cups (355 ml) water
Kosher salt and freshly ground black pepper
1 medium yellow squash, cut into ½-inch (1.3 cm)-thick rounds
1 medium zucchini, cut into ½-inch (1.3 cm)-thick rounds
2 tablespoons (30 ml) avocado or extra-virgin olive oil, divided
1 pound (455 g) flank steak
2 packed cups (40 g) arugula
1½ cups (225 g) cherry tomatoes, halved
1 ear steamed corn, kernels removed
1 recipe Avocado Green Goddess Dressing (page 16)

# Beef and Broccoli Bowls

These bowls are not *that* beef and broccoli. They are so far from it, yet at the same time pull hard on the underlying ingredients, umami-rich, savory flavors, and comfort we associate with that saucy take-out dish. This version is wholesome, nourishing, and packed with lots of green vegetables and herbs. It starts with an underrated and underutilized favorite: broccoli stems. Here, they're processed into rice-like grains and quickly sautéed for a tender bite with a mild-mannered flavor.

**Serves 4**

2½ tablespoons (37 ml) avocado or
   extra-virgin olive oil, divided
1 pound (455 g) ground beef
Kosher salt and freshly ground black
   pepper
1½ tablespoons (23 ml) coconut
   aminos, divided
¼ cup (12 g) chopped Thai basil
16 ounces (455 g) riced broccoli
1 large (or 2 medium) bok choy
2 cloves garlic, minced
1 cup (40 g) shredded radicchio
4 scallions, thinly sliced
Kimchi
Bean sprouts
1 recipe Miso-Ginger Sauce (page 23)
Sesame seeds

1 Heat ½ tablespoon (7 ml) of the oil in a large skillet over medium-high heat. Add the beef, season with salt and pepper, and cook, breaking up the meat with a wooden spoon, until browned and cooked through, 6 to 8 minutes. Stir in 1 tablespoon (15 ml) of the coconut aminos and cook for a minute longer. Remove from the heat and stir in the basil.

2 Meanwhile, heat 1 tablespoon (15 ml) of oil in a separate skillet over medium heat. Add the riced broccoli, salt, and pepper, and cook, stirring occasionally, until the broccoli is slightly softened, 3 to 5 minutes. Divide among bowls.

3 Heat the remaining 1 tablespoon (15 ml) oil in the same skillet, add the bok choy, and toss to coat. Add the garlic and a pinch of salt, and sauté, tossing occasionally, until just wilted. Stir in the remaining ½ tablespoon (7 ml) coconut aminos and cook 1 minute longer.

4 To serve, add the bok choy and radicchio to the bowls with the broccoli. Top with beef, scallions, kimchi, and bean sprouts, drizzle with Miso-Ginger Sauce, and sprinkle with sesame seeds.

**Ingredient Tip!** Riced broccoli is no more than chopped broccoli stems that have been blitzed in the food processor and broken into small "grains" that resemble rice. When making your own (see how on page 12), take a few minutes to peel away the tough outer layer of the stem. It makes a big difference, leaving you with broccoli rice that's tender rather than tough and chewy.

# Korean-Style Beef Bowls with Zucchini Noodles

Inspired by bulgogi, the Korean dish with sliced beef marinated in a subtly sweetened mix of soy sauce, sesame oil, and garlic, this bowl greets you with big flavors and is bound to hit all of your taste buds. It's the whole package of sweet, salty, savory, and spicy. In place of sliced steak, this version opts for quick-cooking ground beef, seared on the stovetop until crispy, then mixed with a savory-sweet sauce.

GLUTEN FREE  |  **Serves 4**

¾ cup (125 g) brown rice
2½ cups (590 ml) water, divided
Kosher salt and freshly ground black
    pepper
1 cup (110 g) shredded carrot
1 cup (235 ml) rice vinegar
2 tablespoons (30 ml) tamari
2 teaspoons (12 g) honey
1 teaspoon (5 ml) toasted sesame oil
¼ teaspoon red pepper flakes
1 pound (455 g) ground beef
2 scallions, thinly sliced
1 tablespoon (15 ml) avocado or
    extra-virgin olive oil
6 packed cups (180 g) baby spinach
2 cloves garlic, minced
8 ounces (225 g) zucchini noodles
Kimchi
1 recipe Miso-Ginger Sauce (page 23)
Sesame seeds

1 Add the rice, 1½ cups (355 ml) of the water, and a generous pinch of salt to a medium saucepan and bring to a boil. Reduce the heat to low, cover, and cook until the rice is tender, about 40 minutes. Remove from the heat and steam the rice with the lid on for 10 minutes.

2 Add the shredded carrots to a medium bowl. Bring the vinegar, remaining 1 cup (235 ml) water, and 1 teaspoon (6 g) of salt to a boil in a medium saucepan, stirring to dissolve the salt. Pour the hot liquid over the carrots; set aside.

3 Whisk together the tamari, honey, sesame oil, and red pepper flakes in a small bowl; set aside.

4 Heat a large skillet over medium-high heat. Add the beef, season with salt and pepper, and cook, breaking up the meat with a wooden spoon, until browned and cooked through, 6 to 8 minutes. Stir in the tamari mixture and scallions, and cook for 1 minute longer.

5 Meanwhile, heat the oil in a separate skillet over medium heat. Add the spinach and garlic, and season with a pinch of salt and pepper. Cook, tossing occasionally, until just wilted, 2 to 3 minutes.

6 Drain the liquid from the carrots. To serve, divide the rice and zucchini noodles among bowls. Top with beef, garlicky spinach, pickled carrots, and kimchi. Drizzle with Miso-Ginger Sauce and sprinkle with sesame seeds.

# Miso Noodle Bowls with Stir-Fried Beef

I've come to learn that a lot of people have *strong* opinions when it comes to marinating beef. Most either sing its praises or are 100 percent against it. I say it all depends on the situation—there's a time and place for marinating. When I'm grilling or searing a good steak I'll always skip it, but I consider it a must any time I'm stir-frying. Allow the slices of sirloin to swim in this soy-ginger marinade for even just 10 minutes and you will be rewarded with the most deeply flavored meat. As with all noodle bowls, particularly when they're made with starchy soba, it's a great idea to toss the hot, off-the-stove noodles with a couple spoonfuls of sauce. Not only will it prevent the noodles from clumping together, but they'll also soak up all the aromas of the sauce.

1 Stir together the soy sauce, garlic, ginger, sesame oil, and cornstarch in a shallow bowl or container until the cornstarch is dissolved. Slice the steak crosswise, against the grain, into ¼-inch (6 mm)-thick strips. Add to the bowl and stir to coat. Marinate for at least 10 minutes.

2 Bring a large pot of salted water to a boil. Add the soba noodles and cook according to the package instructions. In the last 2 minutes of cooking, add the kale, and stir to combine. Drain the noodles and kale, and rinse well with cool water. Toss with 2 tablespoons (30 ml) of the Miso Tahini Sauce.

3 Heat the avocado oil in a large skillet or wok over high heat until very hot but not yet smoking. Add the beef to the skillet in a single layer, working in batches if necessary. Cook undisturbed until the beef begins to brown, 1 to 2 minutes. Toss the beef and stir-fry for about 30 seconds. Transfer to a plate and repeat with the remainder of the beef.

4 To serve, divide the soba noodles and kale among bowls. Top with stir-fried beef, cabbage, and carrots. Drizzle with Miso Tahini Sauce and sprinkle with sesame seeds and red pepper flakes.

**Serves 4**

2 tablespoons (30 ml) soy sauce
1 clove garlic, minced
1 teaspoon (2 g) finely chopped fresh ginger
½ teaspoon toasted sesame oil
½ teaspoon cornstarch
12 ounces (340 g) sirloin steak
Kosher salt and freshly ground pepper
8 ounces (225 g) buckwheat soba noodles
3 cups (210 g) finely shredded Tuscan kale
1 recipe Miso Tahini Sauce (page 26)
1 tablespoon (15 ml) avocado oil, more as needed
2 cups (140 g) finely shredded red cabbage
1 cup (110 g) shredded carrot
Sesame seeds
Red pepper flakes

# Ginger Beef Bowls

Flank steak is my favorite cut of beef for easy weeknight dinners and bowls. It has just enough fat to make it seriously flavorful without being overwhelmingly rich. Get your cast-iron skillet screaming hot, and in 10 minutes' time you've got a well-seared steak with a bright pinkish-red center infused with notes of ginger, sesame, and soy. A handful of sautéed mushrooms add even more meatiness to the bowl, and it gets a nice healthy balance from a trio of bok choy, crisp snow peas, and watermelon radish. If you can't find watermelon radish, substitute a couple of sliced round radishes per bowl.

1 Whisk together the soy sauce, sesame oil, garlic, and ginger in a shallow container. Add the steak, and marinate for at least 30 minutes.

2 Cook the rice noodles according to the package instructions. Drain and set aside.

3 Remove the steak from the marinade, and discard the liquid. Season the steak with salt and pepper. Heat 1 tablespoon (15 ml) of the oil in a cast-iron skillet over medium-high heat until very hot but not smoking. Sear the steak for 5 minutes on each side. Transfer to a cutting board.

4 Heat the remaining 1 tablespoon (15 ml) oil in the same skillet over medium heat. Add the bok choy and mushrooms, season with a pinch of salt, and cook until the greens are just wilted and the mushrooms are soft, about 3 minutes.

5 Slice the steak against the grain into thin slices. To serve, divide the rice noodles, steak, bok choy and mushrooms, snow peas, and radish among bowls. Drizzle with Peanut Sauce and sprinkle with sesame seeds.

**Serves 4**

2 tablespoons (30 ml) soy sauce

1 teaspoon (5 ml) sesame oil

1 clove garlic, minced

1 teaspoon (2 g) finely chopped fresh ginger

1 pound (455 g) flank steak

6 ounces (168 g) vermicelli rice noodles

Kosher salt and freshly ground black pepper

2 tablespoons (30 ml) avocado or extra-virgin olive oil, divided

4 heads baby bok choy, trimmed

4 ounces (115 g) shiitake mushrooms, stemmed and thinly sliced

1 cup (75 g) snow peas

1 watermelon radish, peeled and thinly sliced

¾ cup (180 ml) Peanut Sauce (page 24)

Sesame seeds

# Winter Chili Bowls with Beef, Beans, and Greens

These hot, hearty Buddha bowls are inspired by my husband's signature chili, which I can never get enough of during the winter months. It's loaded with deeply browned ground meat, plenty of beans, and just the right blend of spices to keep it warming and flavorful without too much heat. For this recipe, I'm partial to using a bowl that's deep, rather than shallow and wide, so I can layer the ingredients one on top of the other. With layers of steaming quinoa and hot chili spooned over the baby kale, the greens submit and slowly soften under the heat of the components above.

GLUTEN FREE | **Serves 4**

¾ cup (130 g) tricolor quinoa, rinsed
1½ cups (355 ml) water
Kosher salt and freshly ground black pepper
½ pound (228 g) ground beef
1 (14-ounce, or 392 g) can fire-roasted diced tomatoes
1 cup (200 g) kidney beans, drained and rinsed
2 tablespoons (12 g) chili powder
1 teaspoon (2 g) ground cumin
¼ teaspoon cayenne pepper
2 heaping cups (140 g) chopped baby kale
2 avocados, peeled, pitted, and thinly sliced
4 radishes, thinly sliced
2 scallions, thinly sliced
Greek yogurt

1 Combine the quinoa, water, and a generous pinch of salt in a medium saucepan. Bring to a boil, then cover, reduce the heat to low, and simmer until tender, about 15 minutes. Remove from the heat, and steam with the lid on for about 5 minutes.

2 Heat a large skillet over medium-high heat. Add the beef, season with salt and pepper, and cook, breaking up the meat with a wooden spoon, until browned and cooked through, 6 to 8 minutes. Add the tomatoes, kidney beans, chili powder, cumin, and cayenne pepper, and stir to combine. Cook until the sauce is slightly thickened, about 5 minutes.

3 To serve, divide the kale among bowls. Top with quinoa, beef and beans, avocado, radishes, scallions, and Greek yogurt.

# Greek Power Bowls

This bowl takes the classic components we know and love in Greek salad and transforms them into a meaty meal that is nourishing and truly satisfying, and just a touch indulgent thanks to the Creamy Feta Sauce. Toothsome bulgur, rich in fiber, iron, and magnesium, gives these bowls a hearty base while spiced ground lamb and garlicky chickpeas team up to add a big boost of protein. Unlike the briny, fat feta crumbles you're used to in Greek salad, here they're blended into a thin, pourable sauce that's simple yet irresistible.

1 Combine the bulgur, water, and a pinch of salt in a medium saucepan. Bring to a boil, then reduce the heat to low, cover, and simmer until tender and all the water has been absorbed, 10 to 15 minutes.

2 Heat the oil in a medium skillet over medium heat. Add the onion and garlic, and sauté until soft, about 3 minutes. Add the lamb, season with salt and pepper, and cook, breaking up the meat with a wooden spoon, until browned and cooked through, 6 to 8 minutes. Stir in the oregano, coriander, paprika, and chickpeas, and cook, stirring occasionally, until the spices are fragrant and the chickpeas are heated through, about 3 minutes.

3 To serve, divide the bulgur among bowls. Top with the lamb and chickpea mixture, lettuce, cucumber, tomato, olives, hummus, and Creamy Feta Sauce.

**Serves 4**

1 cup (165 g) bulgur
2 cups (470 ml) water
Kosher salt and freshly ground black pepper
1 tablespoon (15 ml) avocado or extra-virgin olive oil
½ medium red onion, diced
1 clove garlic, minced
½ pound (228 g) ground lamb
1 teaspoon (1 g) dried oregano
1 teaspoon (2 g) ground coriander
½ teaspoon paprika
1 cup (200 g) chickpeas, drained and rinsed
3 cups (165 g) chopped romaine or mixed greens
½ English cucumber, halved and sliced
2 plum tomatoes, chopped
½ cup (50 g) pitted kalamata olives
Hummus
1 recipe Creamy Feta Sauce (page 20)

# Stuffed Eggplant Bowls with Spiced Lamb

Take everything you love about meaty stuffed eggplant filled with an array of spices, then pile on even more fresh veggies, drizzle with Creamy Feta Sauce, and you end up with this wholesome Buddha bowl. While just about any type of multipurpose eggplant will work in this recipe, graffiti eggplant and Italian eggplant are the varieties I prefer because of their reliably smallish size and creamy flesh.

**Serves 4**

2 small eggplants (about 1 pound, or 455 g each)
2 tablespoons (30 ml) avocado or extra-virgin olive oil, divided
Kosher salt and freshly ground black pepper
1 cup (165 g) bulgur
2 cups (470 ml) water
3 packed cups (90 g) baby spinach
¼ cup (12 g) chopped fresh parsley
1 tablespoon (15 ml) freshly squeezed lemon juice
1¼ teaspoons (3 g) ground cumin, divided
½ medium onion, diced
1½ pounds (680 g) ground lamb
1 teaspoon (2 g) ground cinnamon
½ teaspoon allspice
1 tablespoon (15 g) tomato paste
½ cup (120 ml) chicken stock
1 recipe Creamy Feta Sauce (page 20)
Toasted pine nuts

1 Preheat the oven to 400°F (200°C, or gas mark 6).

2 Cut the eggplant in half lengthwise, from stem to tail. Lightly score the flesh on each half, then brush with 1 tablespoon (15 ml) of the oil and sprinkle with salt and pepper. Place on a rimmed baking sheet, cut-side up. Roast until soft and tender, 30 to 35 minutes.

3 Meanwhile, combine the bulgur, water, and a generous pinch of salt in a medium saucepan. Bring to a boil, then cover, reduce the heat to low, and simmer until tender, 10 to 15 minutes. Remove from the heat and stir in the spinach, parsley, lemon juice, and ¼ teaspoon of the cumin.

4 Heat the remaining 1 tablespoon (15 ml) oil in a large skillet over medium heat. Add the onion and cook, stirring occasionally, until soft, about 3 minutes. Add the lamb, season with the remaining 1 teaspoon (2 g) cumin, cinnamon, allspice, salt, and pepper, and cook, breaking up the meat with a wooden spoon, until browned and cooked through, 6 to 8 minutes. Add the tomato paste and stir until the meat is well coated. Stir in the stock, and cook for 2 minutes longer.

5 To serve, divide the bulgur and spinach among bowls. Top with eggplant and lamb. Drizzle with Creamy Feta Sauce and sprinkle with pine nuts.

# Lamb Kebab Bowls

Anytime I'm outside of New York City in the summertime and have the chance to cook on a grill, I jump at the opportunity without hesitation. Grilling is a real treat for a city dweller. First up on the menu are always kebabs—they're my quintessential summer dinner. With thick cubes of garlic- and herb-marinated meat, skewered between an assortment of bright vegetables, they feel light and nourishing, yet hearty and satisfying at the same time. And that's exactly what comes through in this bowl (minus the grill and skewers!). Tender pieces of lamb replace my usual beef sirloin, and the vegetables pick up a light roasted char in the oven.

1 Whisk together 2 tablespoons (30 ml) of the oil, parsley, oregano, lemon juice, garlic, ½ teaspoon salt, and ¼ teaspoon pepper in a medium bowl. Add the lamb and stir until well coated. Cover and marinate in the refrigerator for at least 1 hour.

2 Preheat the oven to 400°F (200°C, or gas mark 6).

3 Toss the onion and zucchini with 1 tablespoon (15 ml) of oil and season with salt and pepper. Arrange in a single layer on a rimmed baking sheet. Roast until tender and lightly browned around the edges, about 20 minutes, stirring once halfway through.

4 Combine the quinoa, water, and a generous pinch of salt in a medium saucepan. Bring to a boil, then cover, reduce the heat to low, and simmer until tender, about 15 minutes. Remove from the heat, and steam with the lid on for about 5 minutes.

5 Meanwhile, heat the remaining 1 tablespoon (15 ml) oil in a large skillet over high heat until very hot but not yet smoking. Add the lamb without crowding the pan, working in batches if necessary. Sear until well browned, 1 to 2 minutes per side.

6 To serve, divide the quinoa and watercress among bowls. Top with lamb, roasted red onion, roasted zucchini, and tomatoes, and drizzle with Raita.

GLUTEN FREE | **Serves 4**

4 tablespoons (60 ml) avocado or
    extra-virgin olive oil, divided
2 tablespoons (12 g) chopped fresh
    parsley
1 tablespoon (6 g) chopped fresh
    oregano
1 tablespoon (15 ml) freshly squeezed
    lemon juice
2 cloves garlic, minced
Kosher salt and freshly ground black
    pepper
1 pound (455 g) boneless lamb leg,
    cut into 1-inch (2.5 cm) cubes
1 medium red onion, cut into large
    pieces
2 medium zucchini, cut into ½-inch
    (1.3 cm)-thick rounds
¾ cup (130 g) quinoa, rinsed
1½ cups (355 ml) water
1 small bunch watercress
2 plum tomatoes, chopped
1 recipe Raita (page 25)

# Lamb Meatball Bowls with Sweet Potato Noodles and Green Tahini

After I got acquainted with the spiralizer, the convenient little kitchen tool that transforms just about any and all vegetables into noodles, spaghetti and meatballs took on a whole new meaning in my house. My favorite iteration is this Middle Eastern spin, with spiced lamb meatballs and spiralized sweet potato noodles. The noodles need just a quick sauté on the stovetop to soften the raw bite.

If you're spiralizing the potatoes at home, two medium potatoes should give you just the right amount of noodles.

**Serves 4**

1 medium red onion, thinly sliced
1 cup (235 ml) white vinegar
1 cup (235 ml) water
Kosher salt and freshly ground black pepper
1 pound (455 g) ground lamb
3 tablespoons (21 g) dried bread-crumbs
2 tablespoons (30 ml) milk
2 cloves garlic, minced
1 tablespoon (15 g) tomato paste
2 teaspoons (4 g) ground cumin
½ teaspoon ground cinnamon
½ teaspoon dried oregano
2 tablespoons (30 ml) extra-virgin olive oil
16 ounces (455 g) sweet potato noodles
2 packed cups (40 g) arugula
1 recipe Green Tahini Sauce (page 26)
Chopped toasted cashews

1 Preheat the oven to 425°F (220°C, or gas mark 7).

2 Add the onion to a medium bowl. Bring the vinegar, water, and 1 teaspoon (6 g) of salt to a boil in a medium saucepan, stirring to dissolve the salt. Pour the hot liquid over the sliced onion; set aside.

3 Add the lamb, breadcrumbs, milk, garlic, tomato paste, cumin, cinnamon, oregano, and ½ teaspoon of salt to a large bowl. Mix with your hands until the ingredients are evenly combined. Do not overwork the meat. Scoop out about 2 tablespoons (30 g) of the mixture and roll into a ball between the palms of your hands. Arrange about 1 inch (2.5 cm) apart on a parchment-lined rimmed baking sheet. Roast until the meatballs are cooked through, about 15 minutes.

4 Meanwhile, heat the oil in a large skillet over medium heat. Add the sweet potato noodles, and season with salt and pepper. Cook, stirring occasionally, until tender, 6 to 8 minutes.

5 To serve, drain the liquid from the onions. Divide the sweet potato noodles among bowls. Top with meatballs, arugula, and pickled red onion. Drizzle with Green Tahini Sauce and sprinkle with cashews.

# Lentil Quinoa Bowls with Harissa Lamb Meatballs

If I could tell you just one thing about this Buddha bowl, I'd want you to know how warm and comforting it is. Harissa lends a hint of heat to the meatballs, which are simmered in a spiced tomatoey broth. Do be sure to coat the meatballs in flour as it's the key to thickening the broth into a velvety sauce.

**1** Preheat the oven to 400°F (200°C, or gas mark 6).

**2** Heat 1 tablespoon (15 ml) of the oil in a Dutch oven over medium heat. Add the onion and cook, stirring occasionally, until soft, about 5 minutes. Add 2 cloves of the garlic, tomato paste, 1 teaspoon (2 g) of cumin, 1½ teaspoons (3 g) of cinnamon, allspice, salt, and pepper, and stir to combine. Cook for another minute then stir in the stock. Bring to a boil, reduce the heat, and simmer while you prepare the meatballs.

**3** Add the remaining garlic, cumin, and cinnamon, plus the bread-crumbs, milk, harissa, and ½ teaspoon of salt, to a large bowl. Stir together until well combined. Add the lamb, and mix until the ingredients are evenly combined. Scoop out about 2 tablespoons (30 g) of the meat and roll into a ball between the palms of your hands. Gently toss the meatballs with flour until coated, then add to the sauce. Cover and simmer over low heat for 30 to 35 minutes.

**4** Toss the beets and broccoli with the remaining 2 tablespoons (30 ml) oil, salt, and pepper. Roast until tender and lightly browned, about 20 minutes, tossing once halfway through.

**5** Combine the quinoa, lentils, water, and a generous pinch of salt in a medium saucepan. Bring to a boil, then cover, reduce the heat to low, and simmer until tender, about 20 minutes. Remove from the heat, cover with a lid, and steam for about 5 minutes.

**6** To serve, divide the Swiss chard among bowls. Top with the quinoa and lentils, meatballs, beets, and broccoli. Spoon the spiced tomato sauce over the top and sprinkle with feta crumbles.

**Serves 4 (about 16 meatballs)**

3 tablespoons (45 ml) avocado or extra-virgin olive oil, divided
½ medium onion, diced
4 cloves garlic, minced, divided
3 tablespoons (45 g) tomato paste
3 teaspoons (6 g) ground cumin, divided
2 teaspoons (4 g) ground cinnamon, divided
½ teaspoon ground allspice
Kosher salt and freshly ground black pepper
3 cups (705 ml) chicken stock
3 tablespoons (21 g) dried bread-crumbs
1 tablespoon (15 ml) milk
2 tablespoons (12 g) harissa
¾ pound (340 g) ground lamb
2 tablespoons (16 g) all-purpose flour
1 small bunch golden beets, peeled and sliced into ¼-inch (6 mm)-thick rounds
½ head broccoli, cut into small florets
½ cup (80 g) red quinoa, rinsed
½ cup (96 g) brown lentils
2 cups (470 ml) water
2 packed cups (140 g) finely shredded Swiss chard
Crumbled feta

# Cauliflower Tabbouleh Bowls with Lamb Meatballs

If you're not yet acquainted with riced cauliflower, these grain-free bowls are a really great place to start. I prefer the convenience of picking up the bagged version in the produce section (typically the same price or less than a head of cauliflower), though you can also make your own by quickly blitzing the florets in small batches in a food processor.

This take on classic tabbouleh salad uses the riced cauliflower as a stand-in for bulgur. The grain-free base along with a mess of herbs and a bold, lemony punch keep the bowls light, while a scoop of lentils ensure a satisfying meal. Serve the bowls warm, or make them in advance and serve cool or at room temperature.

GLUTEN FREE | **Serves 4**

1 pound (455 g) ground lamb
½ cup (24 g) finely chopped fresh parsley, divided
5 tablespoons (15 g) finely chopped fresh mint, divided
1 tablespoon (15 g) tomato paste
2 cloves garlic, minced
2 teaspoons (4 g) ground cumin
Kosher salt and freshly ground black pepper
1 tablespoon (15 ml) extra-virgin olive oil
12 ounces (340 g) riced cauliflower
1 heaping cup (150 g) grape tomatoes, halved
1 medium English cucumber, quartered and chopped
Kalamata olives, pitted
1 recipe Lemon Tahini Sauce (page 26)
Sumac

1 Preheat the oven to 425°F (220°C, or gas mark 7).

2 Add the lamb, ¼ cup (12 g) of the parsley, 2 tablespoons (6 g) of the mint, tomato paste, garlic, cumin, and ½ teaspoon of salt to a large bowl. Mix with your hands until the ingredients are evenly combined. Do not overwork the meat. Scoop out about 2 tablespoons (30 g) of the mixture and roll into a ball between the palms of your hands. Arrange about 1 inch (2.5 cm) apart on a parchment-lined rimmed baking sheet. Roast until the meatballs are cooked through, about 15 minutes.

3 Meanwhile, heat the olive oil in a medium skillet over medium heat. Add the riced cauliflower, season with salt and pepper, and stir to coat with the oil. Cook, stirring occasionally, until the cauliflower is slightly softened, about 3 minutes. Remove from the heat and let cool. Stir in the remaining ¼ cup (12 g) parsley and remaining 3 tablespoons (9 g) mint.

4 To serve, divide the riced cauliflower among bowls. Top with lamb meatballs, tomatoes, cucumber, and olives. Drizzle with Lemon Tahini Sauce and sprinkle with sumac.

# Lamb and Roasted Cauliflower Taco Bowls with Chimichurri

This is one of the best taco bowls I've made in a long, long time. And it's all thanks to stepping slightly outside my comfort zone and building a taco bowl with seared cubes of tender lamb, in place of steak. It has the smoky, earthy undertones you might associate with some Middle Eastern lamb dishes, with a twist of tangy, herb-packed Chimichurri Sauce and creamy avocado.

1 Preheat the oven to 400°F (200°C, or gas mark 6).

2 Add the sliced radishes to a medium bowl. Bring the vinegar, ½ cup (120 ml) of the water, and ½ teaspoon of salt to a boil in a medium saucepan, stirring to dissolve the salt. Pour the hot liquid over the radishes; set aside. Rinse out the saucepan.

3 Toss the cauliflower with 1 tablespoon (15 ml) of the oil, cumin, garlic powder, red pepper flakes, salt, and pepper. Arrange in a single layer on a rimmed baking sheet. Roast until tender and lightly browned, about 20 minutes, stirring once halfway through.

4 Meanwhile, combine the freekeh, remaining 2 cups (470 ml) water, and a generous pinch of salt in a medium saucepan. Bring to a boil, then reduce the heat to low and simmer for 15 minutes, stirring occasionally, until all the liquid has been absorbed and the freekeh is tender. Remove from the heat, cover with a lid, and steam for about 5 minutes.

5 Pat the lamb completely dry, and season all over with the paprika, salt, and pepper. Heat the remaining 1 tablespoon (15 ml) oil in a large skillet over high heat until very hot but not yet smoking. Sear the lamb for 2 minutes on each side.

6 Drain the liquid from the radishes. To serve, divide the freekeh among bowls. Top with roasted cauliflower, lamb, and avocado. Drizzle with Chimichurri Sauce and sprinkle with pumpkin seeds.

**Serves 4**

8 radishes, thinly sliced
½ cup (120 ml) white vinegar
2½ cups (590 ml) water, divided
Kosher salt and freshly ground black pepper
½ head cauliflower, cut into small florets (about 3 cups, or 400 g)
2 tablespoons (30 ml) avocado or extra-virgin olive oil, divided
1 teaspoon (2 g) ground cumin
1 teaspoon (2 g) garlic powder
½ teaspoon red pepper flakes
¾ cup (125 g) cracked freekeh
1 pound (455 g) top round lamb, cut into 1-inch (2.5 cm) cubes
1 teaspoon (2 g) smoked paprika
2 avocados, peeled, pitted, and thinly sliced
1 recipe Chimichurri Sauce (page 19)
Toasted pumpkin seeds

# Vegetable BOWLS

Super Green Quinoa Bowls **116**

Crispy White Bean and Pesto Bowls **117**

Green Goddess Quinoa Bowls with Crispy Tofu **119**

Za'atar Chickpea Bowls **120**

Brown Rice and Kale Pesto Bowls **122**

Cauliflower Falafel Power Bowls **124**

Herbed Chickpea and Bulgur Bowls **125**

Butternut Squash and Kale Bowls **126**

Lentil and Roasted Tomatillo Bowls **127**

Banh Mi Bowls **128**

Thai Coconut Curry Bowls **131**

Vegetarian Sushi Bowls **132**

Spring Soba Bowls **133**

Broccoli Rice and Egg Bowls **134**

Cauliflower Pad Thai Bowls **135**

Spicy Sesame Tofu and Rice Bowls **136**

Chili-Maple Tofu Bowls **139**

Masala Chickpea Bowls **140**

Spiced Bean and Mushroom Bowls with Roasted Red Pepper Sauce **141**

Harvest Macro Bowls **142**

Turmeric-Ginger Cauliflower and Lentil Bowls **143**

Sweet Potato and Lentil Taco Bowls **144**

Chipotle Sweet Potato Bowls **145**

Moroccan-Spiced Chickpea Bowls **146**

Winter Squash and Farro Macro Bowls **149**

Beet Falafel Bowls **150**

Ethiopian-Spiced Red Lentil Bowls with Greens **152**

Turmeric-Roasted Vegetable Bowls **153**

Chili-Lime Portobello Bowls **154**

# Super Green Quinoa Bowls

This is a bowl for those days when you are craving all the greens things. I'm talking about the kind of craving that extends way beyond a salad. Instead, true to its name, this healthy bowl brings together a rainbow of green-hued, roasted, tender, and fresh vegetables.

This recipe also uses one of my favorite quick tricks to mellow the bite of tough greens. Instead of steaming or sautéing into submission, the shredded kale is stirred into the warm, just-cooked quinoa. The residual heat from the grains softens the greens to just the right texture. The same technique works with more delicate greens, like baby spinach and arugula, and leaves them with a nice, warm, wilted texture.

VEGAN · GLUTEN FREE

**Serves 4**

1 head broccoli, cut into florets
2½ tablespoons (37 ml) avocado or extra-virgin olive oil, divided
Kosher salt and freshly ground black pepper
1 cup (175 g) quinoa, rinsed
2 cups (470 ml) water
4 cups (280 g) shredded Tuscan kale
2 medium zucchini, cut into half-moons
1 cup (120 g) shelled edamame
2 avocados, peeled, pitted, and thinly sliced
1 recipe Green Tahini Sauce (page 26)
Hemp seeds

1 Preheat the oven to 400°F (200°C, or gas mark 6).

2 Drizzle the broccoli with 2 tablespoons (30 ml) of the oil, salt, and pepper, and toss to coat. Arrange in a single layer on a rimmed baking sheet. Roast until tender and lightly browned around the tops, about 20 minutes, stirring once halfway through.

3 Meanwhile, combine the quinoa, water, and a generous pinch of salt in a medium saucepan. Bring to a boil, then cover, reduce the heat to low, and simmer until tender, about 15 minutes. Remove from the heat, and steam with the lid on for about 5 minutes.

4 Add the kale to a large bowl, along with the remaining ½ tablespoon (7 ml) oil and cooked quinoa. Stir until well combined. Let sit until the kale softens slightly, about 5 minutes.

5 To serve, divide the quinoa and kale among bowls. Top with roasted broccoli, zucchini, edamame, and avocado. Drizzle with Green Tahini Sauce and sprinkle with hemp seeds.

# Crispy White Bean and Pesto Bowls

Beans and greens are a favorite of mine for quick, simple bowls I can reliably pull together in no time. Mild-mannered, humble white beans, whether canned or dried, are a quick way to give your bowl a boost of protein and versatile enough to be paired with just about everything. Here, they pick up some extra texture when they're tossed with a layer of heart-healthy oil and then added to a screaming-hot skillet and cooked until blistered and crisp. They're partnered with warm lemony kale that has a touch of heat, roasted asparagus, and a fresh, herby pesto to top it off. While I suggest using basil for the pesto, it can really be made with any herbs you have handy.

1 Preheat the oven to 400°F (200°C, or gas mark 6).

2 Combine the barley, water, and a generous pinch of salt in a medium saucepan. Bring to a boil, then cover, reduce the heat to low, and simmer for 15 minutes. Stir in the quinoa, and continue cooking until tender, 15 to 20 minutes longer. Remove from the heat and stir in a spoonful of pesto.

3 Toss the asparagus with 1 tablespoon (15 ml) of the oil, salt, and pepper, and arrange in a single layer on a rimmed baking sheet. Roast until tender, about 15 minutes, stirring once halfway through.

4 Meanwhile, heat 1 tablespoon (15 ml) of oil in a large skillet over medium heat. Add the kale, garlic, red pepper flakes, and salt. Cook, tossing occasionally, until the kale is wilted, about 5 minutes. Remove from the heat and stir in the lemon juice. Transfer to a separate bowl.

5 Add the remaining 1 tablespoon (15 ml) oil to the same skillet and increase the heat to medium-high. Add the beans, season with salt and pepper, and spread in a single layer. Cook undisturbed until browned, about 3 minutes. Stir the beans and cook until lightly browned and blistered, 3 to 4 minutes longer.

6 To serve, divide the grains and kale among bowls. Top with asparagus, crispy white beans, radishes, and Basil Pesto Sauce.

VEGETARIAN | **Serves 4**

½ cup (85 g) pearled barley
2 cups (470 ml) water
Kosher salt and freshly ground black pepper
½ cup (90 g) quinoa, rinsed
1 recipe Basil Pesto Sauce (page 21)
1 bunch asparagus, ends trimmed
3 tablespoons (45 ml) avocado or extra-virgin olive oil, divided
6 cups (420 g) shredded Tuscan kale
2 cloves garlic, minced
¼ teaspoon red pepper flakes
1 tablespoon (15 ml) freshly squeezed lemon juice
1½ cups (300 g) or 1 (15-ounce, or 420 g) can white beans, drained and rinsed
4 radishes, thinly sliced

# Green Goddess Quinoa Bowls with Crispy Tofu

There are times, particularly after travel or a weekend of indulgence, that I find myself craving all the green things. It's my body's plea for a wholesome meal loaded with as many veggies and nourishing ingredients as possible, and these bowls are my favorite solution every time. Filled with a mix of cooked and raw vegetables, like tender steamed broccoli, asparagus ribbons, and crunchy snap peas, plus protein-rich nutty red quinoa and tofu, these bowls are light, yet filling. True to its name, it's finished off with a velvety smooth green goddess dressing that's blended together with avocado, lemon, and a medley of fragrant herbs.

Get a head start by blending together the dressing, cooking the quinoa and tofu, and steaming the broccoli a day in advance, and then reheat just before serving.

1 Combine the quinoa, water, and a generous pinch of salt in a medium saucepan. Bring to a boil, then cover, reduce the heat to low, and simmer until tender, about 15 minutes. Remove from the heat, and steam with the lid on for about 5 minutes.

2 Heat the oil in a large skillet over medium-high heat until shimmering. Add the tofu, season with salt and pepper, and cook until the bottom is lightly browned and crisp, about 2 minutes. Flip and continue cooking until all sides are browned.

3 Meanwhile, steam the broccoli.

4 To serve, stir a spoonful of the sauce into the quinoa, then divide among bowls. Top with tofu, broccoli, asparagus, snap peas, and bean sprouts. Drizzle with Avocado Green Goddess Dressing and sprinkle with hemp seeds.

VEGETARIAN · GLUTEN FREE

**Serves 4**

1 cup (175 g) red quinoa, rinsed
2 cups (470 ml) water
Kosher salt and freshly ground black pepper
1 tablespoon (14 g) coconut oil
14 ounces (392 g) extra-firm tofu, pressed, drained, and cubed
1 medium head broccoli, cut into florets
1 recipe Avocado Green Goddess Dressing (page 16)
12 thick asparagus spears, ends trimmed and shaved into ribbons
6 ounces (168 g) snap peas, halved
Bean sprouts
Hemp seeds

# Za'atar Chickpea Bowls

I think chickpeas are one of the most wonderful staples to keep in your pantry at all times (and because I can't always be counted on to plan ahead, I stick with canned). Their versatility is hard to match and, best of all, they have the most wonderful chameleon-like ability to partner up with any herb, spice, or flavor combination. Here, they're combined with za'atar—the Middle Eastern blend of dried thyme, sumac, and sesame seeds—for a tangy, herbal, nutty pop of flavor with a hint of crunch.

**VEGETARIAN · GLUTEN FREE**

**Serves 4**

4 medium carrots
3 tablespoons (45 ml) avocado or
 extra-virgin olive oil, divided
Kosher salt and freshly ground black
 pepper
1 cup (175 g) quinoa, rinsed
2 cups (470 ml) water
2 teaspoons (10 ml) apple cider
 vinegar
6 cups (420 g) shredded kale, divided
½ yellow onion, diced
1½ cups (300 g) or 1 (15-ounce, or
 420 g) can chickpeas, drained and
 rinsed
2 teaspoons (4 g) za'atar
1 teaspoon (2 g) ground cumin
2 beets, peeled and thinly sliced
¾ cup (180 ml) Cilantro Yogurt Sauce
 (page 27)
Sesame seeds

1 Preheat the oven to 400°F (200°C, or gas mark 6).

2 Peel and cut the carrots into ¼-inch (6 mm)-thick slices. Toss with 1 tablespoon (15 ml) of the oil, salt, and pepper, and arrange in a single layer on a rimmed baking sheet. Roast until tender and browned around the edges, about 20 minutes, flipping over halfway through.

3 Meanwhile, combine the quinoa, water, and a pinch of salt in a medium saucepan. Bring to a boil, then reduce the heat to low, cover, and simmer until tender, about 15 minutes. Remove from the heat, stir in the vinegar and 2 cups (140 g) of the kale, and steam with the lid on for about 5 minutes.

4 Meanwhile, heat the remaining 2 tablespoons (30 ml) oil in a large skillet over medium heat. Add the onion and cook, stirring occasionally, until soft. Stir in the chickpeas, za'atar, cumin, salt, and pepper. Cook, stirring occasionally, until the chickpeas are heated through and fragrant, about 5 minutes.

5 To serve, divide the quinoa among bowls. Top with chickpeas, carrots, the remaining 4 cups (280 g) kale, and sliced beets. Drizzle with Cilantro Yogurt Sauce and sprinkle with sesame seeds.

# Brown Rice and Kale Pesto Bowls

Not too far back, I went to Los Angeles for the first time. At the top of my list was breakfast at Sqirl, where I hoped to try as much of the menu as I could. It exceeded all my expectations, and I came home on a mission to recreate their famed sorrel pesto rice bowl as soon as possible. While this bowl does indeed start with nutty brown rice mixed and topped with pesto (one that's lemony and made with kale), and gets topped with an egg, it is more of a loosely inspired version than an exact recreation.

VEGETARIAN · GLUTEN FREE

**Serves 4**

1 cup (235 ml) white vinegar
2½ cups (590 ml) water, divided
Kosher salt and freshly ground black pepper
½ cup (80 g) thinly sliced red onion
¾ cup (125 g) brown rice
2 cups (140 g) chopped kale leaves, stems removed
2 tablespoons (18 g) unsalted pistachios
2 tablespoons (10 g) grated Pecorino cheese
1 clove garlic
5 tablespoons (75 ml) extra-virgin olive oil, divided
2 tablespoons (30 ml) freshly squeezed lemon juice
1 bunch asparagus, ends trimmed
1 small head cauliflower, cut into florets
2 teaspoons (4 g) ground turmeric
4 eggs, poached

1 Preheat the oven to 400°F (200°C, or gas mark 6).

2 Bring the vinegar, 1 cup (235 ml) of the water, and 1 teaspoon (6 g) of salt to a boil in a medium saucepan, stirring to dissolve the salt. Pour the hot liquid over the red onion in a small bowl; set aside.

3 Rinse out the saucepan. Add the rice, remaining 1½ cups (355 ml) water, and a generous pinch of salt, and bring to a boil. Reduce the heat to low, cover, and cook until the rice is tender, about 40 minutes. Remove from the heat, and steam the rice with the lid on for 10 minutes.

4 Place the kale, pistachios, cheese, garlic, and salt in the bowl of a food processor or blender. Process until finely chopped, about 1 minute. Scrape down the sides of the bowl, as necessary. With the machine running, stream in 3 tablespoons (45 ml) of the oil and lemon juice, blending until the pesto looks uniform; set aside.

5 Toss the asparagus with 1 tablespoon (15 ml) of oil, salt, and pepper. Spread in an even layer on a rimmed baking sheet. Toss the cauliflower with the remaining 1 tablespoon (15 ml) oil, turmeric, salt, and pepper. Spread in an even layer on a separate rimmed baking sheet. Roast until the vegetables are tender and lightly browned around the edges, about 20 minutes, stirring once halfway through.

6 To serve, drain the liquid from the onions. Stir a spoonful of the pesto into the rice, then divide the rice among bowls. Top each bowl with asparagus, cauliflower, pickled red onions, and an egg, then spoon extra pesto on top.

# Cauliflower Falafel Power Bowls

This nourishing bowl is exactly how I like to eat falafel—paired with a generous helping of fresh vegetables, creamy avocado, a scoop of hummus, and something tangy, which in this case is red cabbage sauerkraut. The most important thing I learned the first time I made baked falafel at home was how surprisingly versatile and easy it is to make. The patties are filling but not too dense, and bake up with a delicate crisp over the exterior. Get a head start by making the falafel up to a couple of days in advance and storing the cooked patties in the fridge, or in the freezer for up to a few months.

**VEGAN | Serves 4**

3 cups or 2 (15-ounce, or 420 g) cans chickpeas, drained and rinsed
1 small red onion, roughly chopped
2 cloves garlic
2 tablespoons (30 ml) freshly squeezed lemon juice
½ packed cup (24 g) fresh parsley leaves
½ packed cup (8 g) fresh cilantro leaves
2 teaspoons (4 g) ground cumin
1 teaspoon (2 g) ground coriander
⅛ teaspoon cayenne pepper
Kosher salt and freshly ground black pepper
3 tablespoons (24 g) all-purpose flour
1 teaspoon (5 g) baking powder
1 tablespoon (15 ml) avocado or extra-virgin olive oil
16 ounces (455 g) riced cauliflower
2 teaspoons (4 g) za'atar
2 packed cups (40 g) arugula
1 medium red bell pepper, cored and chopped
2 avocados, peeled, pitted, and diced
Red cabbage or beet sauerkraut
Hummus

1 If using dried beans, add the chickpeas to a medium bowl and cover with water by at least 1 inch (2.5 cm). Let them sit, uncovered, at room temperature for 24 hours.

2 Preheat the oven to 375°F (190°C, or gas mark 5).

3 Add the drained chickpeas, onion, garlic, lemon juice, parsley, cilantro, cumin, coriander, cayenne, 1 teaspoon (6 g) of salt, and ¼ teaspoon pepper to the bowl of a food processor. Pulse about 10 times until the chickpeas are chopped. Scrape down the sides of the bowl, add the flour and baking powder, and pulse until the mixture is well combined.

4 Scoop out about 2 tablespoons of the mixture and roll it into a ball in the palms of your hands. Transfer to a lightly greased baking sheet and use a spatula to flatten into a ½-inch (1.3 cm)-thick disk. Repeat with the remainder of the mixture.

5 Bake the falafel until cooked through and tender, 25 to 30 minutes, flipping once halfway through.

6 Heat the oil in a large skillet over medium heat. Add the riced cauliflower, za'atar, salt, and pepper, and stir to combine. Cook, stirring occasionally, until the cauliflower is slightly softened, about 3 minutes.

7 To serve, divide the cauliflower rice and arugula among bowls. Top with falafel patties, bell pepper, avocado, sauerkraut, and a scoop of hummus.

# Herbed Chickpea and Bulgur Bowls

Get a head start on prepping the chickpeas in this recipe and you will be handsomely rewarded. They're tossed with a simple mix of oil, red onion, fresh herbs, and tangy sumac, then left to marinade for as much time as you can spare. When I remember to plan ahead, I'll take a few minutes to mix these ingredients together a full day, or even two, ahead of time. The result is a deep melding of earthy, bright, fresh flavors that have really worked themselves into the chickpeas. But, the result is still quite delicious when prepared shortly before eating.

1 Add the chickpeas, oil, onion, herbs, sumac, salt, and pepper to a medium bowl, and stir to combine. Set aside to marinate while you prepare the remainder of the bowl.

2 Combine the bulgur, water, and a generous pinch of salt in a medium saucepan. Bring to a boil, then cover, reduce the heat to low, and simmer until tender, 10 to 15 minutes. Remove from the heat and stir in the arugula and vinegar.

3 Meanwhile, steam the broccoli.

4 To serve, divide the bulgur and cabbage among bowls. Top with chickpeas, broccoli, avocado, and Roasted Red Pepper Sauce.

**VEGAN | Serves 4**

1½ cups (300 g) or 1 (15-ounce, or 420 g) can chickpeas, drained and rinsed

1 tablespoon (15 ml) avocado or extra-virgin olive oil

¼ cup (40 g) diced red onion

2 tablespoons (6 g) finely chopped parsley

1 tablespoon (1 g) finely chopped cilantro

½ teaspoon sumac

Kosher salt and freshly ground black pepper

¾ cup (125 g) bulgur

1½ cups (355 ml) water

2 packed cups (40 g) arugula

2 teaspoons (10 ml) apple cider vinegar

½ head broccoli, cut into small florets

2 cups (140 g) finely shredded red cabbage

2 avocados, peeled, pitted, and thinly sliced

¾ cup (180 ml) Roasted Red Pepper Sauce (page 25)

# Butternut Squash and Kale Bowls

Let's call this recipe what it really is—fall in a bowl. It is one wildly delicious Buddha bowl, packed with everything I adore about fresh fall food. From sweet winter squash to crispy Brussels sprouts, freshly picked crisp apple, and bitter radicchio, this bowl has it all. It comes together in a beautiful rainbow of colors, and is the perfect balance of sweet, earthy, and slightly bitter flavors. Because the ingredients, even the greens, are so hearty, this is a recipe I love making in advance and packing for lunch. Just wait to add the sauce and crispy chickpeas until you're ready to eat.

VEGAN | **Serves 4**

½ cup (82 g) pearled farro
1¼ cups (295 ml) water
Kosher salt and freshly ground black pepper
1 small butternut squash, peeled and cut into ½-inch (1.3 cm)-thick batons
1 pound (455 g) Brussels sprouts, trimmed and halved
2 tablespoons (30 ml) avocado, coconut, or extra-virgin olive oil
3 cups (360 g) steamed kale
1 cup (40 g) shredded radicchio
1 firm apple, cored and diced
Crispy chickpeas
1 recipe Spicy Maple Tahini Sauce (page 26)

1 Preheat the oven to 425°F (220°C, or gas mark 7).

2 Add the farro, water, and a generous pinch of salt to a medium saucepan. Bring to a boil, then reduce the heat to low, cover, and simmer until the farro is tender with a slight chew, about 30 minutes.

3 Meanwhile, toss the squash and Brussels sprouts with the oil, salt, and pepper. Spread in a single layer on a rimmed baking sheet. Roast until the squash is tender and the Brussels sprouts are browned and crispy, about 20 minutes, stirring once halfway through.

4 To serve, divide the kale among bowls. Top with squash, Brussels sprouts, farro, radicchio, and apple. Sprinkle with crispy chickpeas and drizzle with Spicy Maple Tahini Sauce.

# Lentil and Roasted Tomatillo Bowls

This is a bowl for salsa verde lovers, for anyone who's dreamed of a less messy way to eat lentil tacos, and for those like me, who never cease to overstuff a tortilla with all the vegetables in sight. While you could certainly use your favorite jar of salsa verde, you should make this warm version if you have the time. It starts by charring the tomatillos, poblano, and garlic under the broiler to bring an extra deep flavor and smokiness to the sauce. It keeps well in the fridge and can be made up to a few days in advance, or stored in the freezer for several months.

1 Set the oven to broil.

2 Place the tomatillos, poblano, and garlic on a rimmed baking sheet, drizzle with 1 tablespoon (15 ml) of the oil, and toss to combine. Broil until the tomatillos are soft with some charred spots, about 8 minutes total. Cool completely. Reduce the oven temperature to 400°F (200°C, or gas mark 6).

3 Add the tomatillos, poblano, garlic, cilantro, and salt to the bowl of a food processor or a blender. Blend continuously until the tomatillos are pureed and the sauce is well combined.

4 Bring the vinegar, ½ cup (120 ml) of the water, and ½ teaspoon salt to a boil in a medium saucepan. Pour the hot liquid over the radishes in a medium bowl; set aside.

5 Rinse out the saucepan. Combine the lentils, remaining 2 cups (470 ml) water, and a pinch of salt in the same saucepan. Bring to a boil, then reduce the heat so the liquid is at a bare simmer. Cook until the lentils are tender, 20 to 30 minutes. Drain and set aside. Meanwhile, prepare the vegetables.

6 Toss the broccoli with the remaining 1 tablespoon (15 ml) oil and arrange in an even layer on a rimmed baking sheet. Roast until tender and lightly browned, about 20 minutes, stirring once halfway through.

7 To serve, drain the liquid from the radishes. Divide the lentils among bowls. Top with radishes, broccoli, corn, and avocado, and drizzle the tomatillo sauce over the top.

**VEGAN · GLUTEN FREE**

**Serves 4**

3 medium tomatillos, husked and washed
½ poblano pepper, seeded
2 cloves garlic
2 tablespoons (30 ml) extra-virgin olive oil, divided
¼ cup (4 g) fresh cilantro
Kosher salt
½ cup (120 ml) white vinegar
2½ cups (590 ml) water, divided
8 radishes, thinly sliced
1 cup (190 g) French lentils, rinsed
1 head broccoli, cut into florets
1 cup (120 g) corn kernels
2 avocados, peeled, pitted, and thinly sliced

# Banh Mi Bowls

I fell even more in love with banh mi sandwiches after savoring them from the small shops tucked along the bustling streets of Hanoi, and then from the local vendors in the Vietnamese coastal city of Hoi An. The confluence of tangy, spicy flavors and textures from the pickled vegetables, fresh herbs, and creamy spread shine through in these bowls, just as much as they do in the classic Vietnamese sandwich. Cubes of tofu are infused with a soy-lemongrass marinade, before being crisped and topped on a bed of floral jasmine rice, alongside a mess of pickled vegetables and crunchy radishes. Protein-rich Greek yogurt replaces mayonnaise as the main ingredient for the creamy sauce, and gets blended with Sriracha for a spicy kick.

The majority of the components in this bowl can be made in advance, with the pickled vegetables and Spicy Yogurt Sauce being prepped up to several days ahead, then stored in the refrigerator.

**VEGETARIAN** | **Serves 4**

14 ounces (392 g) extra-firm tofu, pressed and drained
2 tablespoons (30 ml) soy sauce
2 teaspoons (10 ml) toasted sesame oil
2 bulbs lemongrass, minced
2 cloves garlic, minced
2 medium carrots, peeled and shaved into ribbons
1 small daikon, peeled and shaved into ribbons
1 cup (235 ml) rice vinegar
3 cups (705 ml) water, divided
Kosher salt and freshly ground black pepper
1 cup (165 g) jasmine rice
2 cups (110 g) chopped romaine lettuce
8 radishes, thinly sliced
¼ cup (4 g) fresh cilantro
½ cup (120 ml) Spicy Yogurt Sauce (page 27)

1 Preheat the oven to 400°F (200°C, or gas mark 6).

2 Cut the tofu into triangles. Whisk together the soy sauce, sesame oil, lemongrass, and garlic in a shallow container. Add the tofu, stir to coat, and marinate for at least 10 minutes.

3 Meanwhile, add the carrots and daikon to a large bowl. Bring the vinegar, 1 cup (235 ml) of the water, and 1 teaspoon (6 g) salt to a boil in a medium saucepan, stirring to dissolve the salt. Pour the hot liquid over the carrots and daikon; set aside.

4 Rinse out the saucepan. Add the rice, remaining 2 cups (470 ml) water, and a generous pinch of salt, and bring to a boil. Reduce the heat, cover, and cook until the rice is tender, about 15 minutes. Remove from the heat, and steam the rice with the lid on for 10 minutes.

5 Meanwhile cook the tofu. Arrange the tofu in a single layer on a large, parchment-lined, rimmed baking sheet, and discard the remaining marinade. Cook until the bottom of the tofu is lightly browned, about 12 minutes. Flip the tofu and cook for another 12 minutes.

6 To serve, drain the liquid from the carrots and daikon. Divide the rice and romaine among bowls. Top with tofu, pickled vegetables, radishes, and cilantro, and drizzle with Spicy Yogurt Sauce.

# Thai Coconut Curry Bowls

There are some recipes that will win you over with a medley of big, bold, savory flavors, and some that will do it purely on looks alone. This Thai-inspired veggie bowl does both, and it does it so well. It's a more vibrant version of the quick red Thai curry my husband and I so often pull together on weeknights when we're craving comfort and a big dose of veggies. Instead of using rice or noodles, I love filling these bowls with a base of fresh zucchini noodles to balance the richness of the coconut milk. The spiced curry broth is packed with the aroma of garlic, ginger, lemongrass, and lime in every bite. It's worth noting that most, though not all, brands of red Thai curry paste contain shellfish. I always use the Thai Kitchen brand, which is vegan and shellfish free.

1 Heat the oil in a medium saucepan over medium heat. Add the garlic and ginger, stir to coat, and cook until fragrant, about 30 seconds. Stir in the curry paste and cook for 1 minute longer. Stir in the coconut milk, stock, and lime zest, and season with salt and pepper. Bring to a boil, then reduce the heat to low and simmer for 15 minutes. Stir in the tofu and green beans, and simmer for 5 minutes longer. Remove from the heat, stir in the tamari, and season to taste.

2 Meanwhile, steam the broccoli.

3 To serve, divide the zucchini noodles among bowls. Top with tofu and green beans, broccoli, and cabbage. Pour the curry sauce over the top, sprinkle with peanuts and cilantro, and add a squeeze of lime juice.

VEGAN · GLUTEN FREE

**Serves 4**

1 tablespoon (14 g) coconut oil
3 cloves garlic, minced
1½ tablespoons (9 g) finely chopped fresh ginger
2 tablespoons (30 g) red Thai curry paste
1 (14-ounce, or 392 g) can unsweetened coconut milk
1½ cups (355 ml) vegetable stock
1 lime, zested, then cut into wedges
Kosher salt and freshly ground black pepper
14 ounces (392 g) extra-firm tofu, pressed, drained, and cubed
8 ounces (225 g) green beans, trimmed
2 teaspoons (10 ml) tamari
1 head broccoli, cut into florets
16 ounces (455 g) zucchini noodles
1 cup (70 g) shredded red cabbage
Roasted unsalted peanuts, chopped
Chopped fresh cilantro

# Vegetarian Sushi Bowls

If you are skilled in making sushi at home, I salute you. I am not. Not even close. And that is just fine by me, because I'm happy to pile all the ingredients from my favorite veggie rolls (plus some extras!) into a big bowl drizzled with a creamy Miso-Ginger Sauce and topped with shredded nori and crunchy sesame seeds. A great tactic to keep veggie-heavy bowls, like this one, interesting is by choosing a mix of ingredients with varied textures: some crisp, others crunchy, and some soft. It's also fun to change things up by using a vegetable peeler to shave the carrots in this bowl into ribbons.

VEGETARIAN | **Serves 4**

1 cup (165 g) brown rice
2 cups (470 ml) plus 2 tablespoons (30 ml) water, divided
Kosher salt and freshly ground black pepper
14 ounces (392 g) extra-firm tofu, pressed and drained
¼ cup (60 ml) soy sauce
2 tablespoons (30 ml) rice vinegar
1 teaspoon (6 g) honey
2 cloves garlic, minced
2 medium carrots, peeled and shaved into ribbons
½ seedless cucumber, thinly sliced
2 avocados, peeled, pitted, and thinly sliced
2 scallions, thinly sliced
Shredded nori
Sesame seeds
1 recipe Miso-Ginger Sauce (page 23)

1 Preheat the oven to 400°F (200°C, or gas mark 6).

2 Add the rice, 2 cups (470 ml) of the water, and a generous pinch of salt to a medium saucepan, and bring to a boil. Reduce the heat to low, cover, and cook until the rice is tender, 40 to 45 minutes. Remove from the heat, and steam the rice with the lid on for 10 minutes.

3 Meanwhile, cut the tofu into triangles. Whisk together the soy sauce, rice vinegar, remaining 2 tablespoons (30 ml) water, honey, and garlic in a shallow container. Add the tofu, stir gently to combine, and marinate for at least 10 minutes.

4 Arrange the tofu in a single layer on a rimmed baking sheet, and discard the remaining marinade. Cook until the bottom of the tofu is lightly browned, about 12 minutes. Flip the tofu and cook for another 12 minutes.

5 To serve, divide the rice among bowls. Top with tofu, carrot, cucumber, and avocado. Garnish with scallions, nori, and sesame seeds, and drizzle with Miso-Ginger Sauce.

# Spring Soba Bowls

When the cold chill of winter finally lifts, some people look forward to the warmer temperatures and tucking their puffy coats into the back of the closet once and for all. But for me, it's all about the arrival of fresh and vibrant spring produce that slowly but surely works its way into the farmers' market. After a long winter filled with root vegetables, it feels nearly impossible to contain my excitement and restrain myself from filling my tote with a little bit of everything.

Arranged around a small pile of nutty soba noodles, this bowl is a celebration of spring. It combines a medley of roasted, sautéed, and crisp seasonal vegetables, topped off with a jammy soft-boiled egg and a light, herby goat cheese sauce.

1 Preheat the oven to 400°F (200°C, or gas mark 6).

2 Arrange the asparagus on a rimmed baking sheet. Drizzle with 1 tablespoon (15 ml) of the oil, salt, and pepper, and stir to coat. Cook until tender and lightly browned, 15 minutes, stirring once halfway through.

3 Meanwhile, heat the remaining 1 tablespoon (15 ml) oil in a large skillet over medium heat. Add the mushrooms and sauté until tender. Stir in the coconut aminos and cook for 1 minute longer.

4 Bring a large pot of salted water to a boil. Add the soba noodles and cook according to the package instructions. Drain and rinse well with cool water.

5 Bring a separate saucepan of water to a boil over medium heat. Use a spoon to carefully lower the eggs into the water. Cook for 6 minutes, maintaining a gentle boil. Reduce the heat if necessary. Transfer the eggs to an ice bath, until they're cool enough to handle but still warm. Peel the eggs, and slice each one in half.

6 To serve, divide the soba noodles among bowls. Top with asparagus, mushrooms, peas, carrots, sliced radish, scallions, and a soft-boiled egg. Drizzle with Herbed Goat Cheese Sauce and sprinkle with sesame seeds.

VEGETARIAN · GLUTEN FREE

**Serves 4**

1 bunch asparagus, ends trimmed
2 tablespoons (30 ml) avocado or extra-virgin olive oil, divided
Kosher salt and freshly ground black pepper
8 ounces (225 g) mixed mushrooms, such as shiitake and cremini, sliced
1 tablespoon (15 ml) coconut aminos
4 ounces (115 g) buckwheat soba noodles
4 large eggs
1 cup (120 g) English peas, blanched
4 medium carrots, peeled and shaved into ribbons
1 watermelon radish, thinly sliced
2 scallions, green parts only, julienned
1 recipe Herbed Goat Cheese Sauce (page 22)
Sesame seeds

# Broccoli Rice and Egg Bowls

This is a recipe dedicated to all my fellow broccoli lovers. You know who you are—you are the adventurous ones who look beyond the florets, and find all the ways you can to work those crisp stems onto your plate. Shredded broccoli slaw is a good place to start, but riced broccoli is my favorite. Made from mostly the stems, this gluten-free grain alternative can really be used just like you'd use rice, quinoa, farro, or other grains. You can find it in the produce section of some stores; otherwise, it's easy to make at home (see page 12 for complete instructions on how to do it).

Riced cauliflower, beets, or sweet potatoes all make a fine substitution for this recipe if you can't find riced broccoli.

**VEGETARIAN · GLUTEN FREE**

**Serves 4**

1 cup (235 ml) white vinegar
1 cup (235 ml) water
Kosher salt and freshly ground black
   pepper
6 radishes, thinly sliced
3 tablespoons (45 ml) avocado or
   extra-virgin olive oil, divided
16 ounces (455 g) riced broccoli
2 cloves garlic, minced
1 teaspoon (2 g) za'atar
4 cups (120 g) baby spinach
1 tablespoon (15 ml) freshly squeezed
   lemon juice
4 large eggs
Crumbled feta
1 recipe Lemon Tahini Sauce (page 26)
Red pepper flakes

1 Bring the vinegar, water, and 1 teaspoon (6 g) of salt to a boil in a medium saucepan, stirring to dissolve the salt. Pour the hot liquid over the radishes in a large bowl; set aside.

2 Heat 1 tablespoon (15 ml) of the oil in a large skillet over medium heat until shimmering. Add the riced broccoli, garlic, za'atar, salt, and pepper. Cook, stirring occasionally, until the broccoli is slightly softened, 3 to 5 minutes. Divide among bowls.

3 Heat 1 tablespoon (15 ml) of oil in the same skillet over medium heat. Add the spinach and season with salt and pepper. Cook, tossing occasionally, until wilted, 2 to 3 minutes. Remove from the heat and stir in the lemon juice. Divide among bowls.

4 Heat the remaining 1 tablespoon (15 ml) oil in the same skillet, and fry the eggs.

5 Drain the liquid from the radishes. To serve, top the riced broccoli and spinach with an egg, radishes, and feta. Drizzle with Lemon Tahini Sauce and sprinkle with red pepper flakes.

# Cauliflower Pad Thai Bowls

For better or worse, there is a tiny neighborhood Thai restaurant around the corner from my apartment that can have a really delicious carton of pad Thai ready for me to pick up within minutes of my call. Recently, I've started taking matters into my own hands when a craving for pad Thai creeps in (which is often!). This veggie-heavy bowl is loaded with so many of the flavors and ingredients that make the take-out version so good, though it is so much healthier. Riced cauliflower takes the place of chewy rice noodles, and is then partnered with crispy tofu and a mess of crisp and vibrant vegetables. Riced broccoli also makes a wonderful substitute for the cauliflower.

1 Heat 1 tablespoon (15 ml) of the oil in a large skillet over medium-high heat. Add the tofu, season with salt and pepper, and cook, flipping occasionally, until all sides are crisp and golden brown. Transfer the tofu to a paper towel–lined plate.

2 Heat the remaining 1 tablespoon (15 ml) oil in the same skillet over medium heat. Add the riced cauliflower and garlic. Cook, stirring occasionally, until the cauliflower is slightly softened, about 3 minutes. Move the cauliflower to one side of the skillet. Pour the eggs into the empty side and scramble until cooked. Mix with the cauliflower rice. Remove from the heat and stir in about 2 tablespoons (30 ml) of the sauce.

3 To serve, divide the cauliflower rice among bowls. Top with tofu, cabbage, carrots, bean sprouts, and cilantro. Garnish with scallions and peanuts, and drizzle with Tamarind Peanut Sauce.

**Serves 4**

2 tablespoons (30 ml) avocado or extra-virgin olive oil, divided
14 ounces (392 g) extra-firm tofu, pressed, drained, and cubed
Kosher salt and freshly ground black pepper
16 ounces (455 g) riced cauliflower
2 cloves garlic, minced
2 large eggs, lightly beaten
¾ cup (180 ml) Tamarind Peanut Sauce (page 24)
1 cup (70 g) shredded red cabbage
1 cup (110 g) shredded carrots
1 cup (100 g) bean sprouts
½ cup (8 g) fresh cilantro leaves
2 scallions, green parts only, thinly sliced
Chopped roasted, unsalted peanuts

# Spicy Sesame Tofu and Rice Bowls

I often find that making just a couple of small, simple changes in the way I prepare ingredients can have very powerful results. Here it's as simple as using a vegetable peeler to shave carrots into thin, pliable ribbons instead of cutting them; roasting broccoli with a drizzle of nutty sesame oil and pungent ginger, for a kick; and filling the bowl with rich, inky-hued forbidden rice, in place of oft-used brown or jasmine rice.

**Serves 4**

¾ cup (125 g) forbidden rice
1½ cups (355 ml) water
Kosher salt
14 ounces (392 g) extra-firm tofu,
    pressed and drained
2 tablespoons (30 ml) tamari
3 tablespoons (45 ml) toasted sesame
    oil, divided
1 teaspoon (6 g) honey
½ teaspoon sambal olek
1 medium head broccoli, cut into
    small florets
½ tablespoon (3 g) finely grated fresh
    ginger
2 medium carrots, peeled and shaved
    into ribbons
2 avocados, peeled, pitted, and thinly
    sliced
Sesame seeds
1 recipe Peanut Sauce (page 24)

1 Preheat the oven to 400°F (200°C, or gas mark 6).

2 Combine the rice, water, and a generous pinch of salt in a medium saucepan and bring to a boil. Reduce the heat to low, cover, and simmer, stirring occasionally, until the rice is tender, about 30 minutes. Meanwhile, prepare the tofu and vegetables.

3 Cut the tofu into triangles. Whisk together the tamari, 1 tablespoon (15 ml) of the sesame oil, honey, and sambal olek in a shallow container. Add the tofu, stir to coat, and marinate for at least 10 minutes.

4 Arrange the tofu in a single layer on one side of a large, parchment-lined, rimmed baking sheet, and discard the remaining marinade. Toss the broccoli with the remaining 2 tablespoons (30 ml) sesame oil, ginger, and salt. Arrange in a single layer on the other half of the baking sheet.

5 Cook until the bottom of the tofu is lightly browned, about 12 minutes. Flip the tofu, stir the broccoli, and cook for another 12 minutes.

6 To serve, divide the rice among bowls. Top with tofu, roasted broccoli, shaved carrots, and avocado. Sprinkle with sesame seeds and drizzle with Peanut Sauce.

**Make It Vegan** | By simply swapping the honey for agave syrup, this recipe easily becomes vegan-friendly. Don't skip the sweetener altogether, as it's essential in keeping the marinade balanced.

# Chili-Maple Tofu Bowls

This Buddha bowl is a testament to exactly what I crave in a really good meal—lots of eye-catching colors, a mix of different textures, and, most of all, a mix of balanced, bright flavors that will awaken your taste buds. It's just the right balance of sweet, spicy, and tangy with earthy, creamy elements to keep it in check. The level of heat is really up to you, as much of it comes from the Spicy Peanut Sauce. I call for Sriracha to spice up the sauce, though you can certainly use garlic chili sauce or sambal olek, and can alter the amount you use based on preference. All of the ingredients can be prepped and cooked in advance, but just wait until right before serving to add the sauce.

1 Bring the vinegar, water, red pepper flakes, and 1 teaspoon (6 g) salt to a boil in a medium saucepan, stirring to dissolve the salt. Pour the hot liquid over the carrots in a medium bowl; set aside.

2 Whisk together the tamari, maple syrup, and garlic chili sauce in a shallow container. Add the tofu and stir to coat. Marinate for at least 10 minutes.

3 Bring a large pot of salted water to a boil. Add the soba noodles and cook according to the package instructions. Drain and rinse well with cool water.

4 Drain the marinade from the tofu. Heat the oil in a large skillet over medium-high heat until shimmering. Add the tofu, season with salt and pepper, and cook until the bottom is lightly browned and crisp, about 2 minutes. Flip and continue cooking until all sides are lightly browned.

5 To serve, drain the liquid from the carrots. Divide the soba noodles among bowls. Top with tofu wedges, pickled carrot ribbons, red cabbage, edamame, and avocado. Drizzle with Spicy Peanut Sauce and sprinkle with scallions.

**VEGAN**

**Serves 4**

1 cup (235 ml) rice vinegar
1 cup (235 ml) water
¼ teaspoon red pepper flakes
Kosher salt and freshly ground black pepper
3 medium carrots, peeled and shaved into ribbons
¼ cup (60 ml) tamari
2 tablespoons (30 ml) maple syrup
2 teaspoons (10 ml) garlic chili sauce
14 ounces (392 g) extra-firm tofu, pressed, drained, and cut into triangles
8 ounces (225 g) buckwheat soba noodles
1 tablespoon (15 ml) avocado or extra-virgin olive oil
1 cup (70 g) finely shredded red cabbage
1 cup (120 g) shelled edamame
2 avocados, peeled, pitted, and thinly sliced
¾ cup (180 ml) Spicy Peanut Sauce (page 24)
3 scallions, green parts only, thinly sliced

# Masala Chickpea Bowls

Garam masala, the staple spice blend in Indian cooking, literally means "warm spice." So it should come as no surprise that when it's mixed into the saucy blend of tomatoes and chickpeas it instantly infuses a deep, warming aroma into this recipe. Not to worry, though—garam masala isn't a spice that packs a lot of heat. The blends can vary here and there, but it's most commonly composed of cinnamon, cardamom, cloves, cumin, coriander, nutmeg, and peppercorns. Should you want a little heat in your Buddha bowl, go ahead and mix in the diced chile.

**VEGETARIAN · GLUTEN FREE**

**Serves 4**

1 small head cauliflower, cut into florets

3 medium carrots, peeled and cut into ¼-inch (6 mm)-thick slices

4 tablespoons (60 ml) avocado or extra-virgin olive oil, divided

Kosher salt and freshly ground black pepper

1 small onion, diced

2 cloves garlic, minced

1 tablespoon (6 g) finely grated fresh ginger

1 small Serrano chile, seeded and diced (optional)

2 teaspoons (4 g) garam masala

1 teaspoon (2 g) ground coriander

½ teaspoon ground turmeric

1 (14-ounce, or 392 g) can diced tomatoes

1½ cups (300 g) or 1 (15-ounce, or 420 g) can chickpeas, drained and rinsed

½ cup (90 g) millet

1¼ cups (295 ml) water

4 cups (280 g) chopped Swiss chard

1 recipe Cilantro Yogurt Sauce (page 27)

**1** Preheat the oven to 400°F (200°C, or gas mark 6).

**2** Toss the cauliflower and carrots with 2 tablespoons (30 ml) of the oil, salt, and pepper. Spread in an even layer on a rimmed baking sheet. Roast for 20 minutes, stirring once halfway through.

**3** Heat 1 tablespoon (15 ml) oil in a large skillet over medium heat. Add the onion, season with salt and pepper, and cook, stirring occasionally, until soft, about 5 minutes. Add the garlic, ginger, Serrano chile (if using), garam masala, coriander, and turmeric, and stir to combine. Cook until fragrant, about 2 minutes. Stir in the tomatoes, chickpeas, and another pinch of salt and pepper. Bring to a boil, then reduce the heat and simmer for 15 minutes, stirring occasionally. Meanwhile, prepare the millet.

**4** Add the millet to a large, dry saucepan and toast over medium heat until golden brown, 4 to 5 minutes. Pour in the water and a generous pinch of salt. The water will sputter at first but will settle quickly. Bring to a boil. Reduce the heat to low, cover, and simmer until most of the water is absorbed, about 15 minutes. Remove from the heat and steam in the pot for 5 minutes.

**5** Heat the remaining 1 tablespoon (15 ml) oil in a skillet over medium heat. Add the chard, season lightly with salt and pepper, and toss to coat with the oil. Cook until tender, 3 to 5 minutes.

**6** To serve, divide the millet and chard among bowls. Top with chickpeas and tomatoes, roasted cauliflower and carrots, and Cilantro Yogurt Sauce.

# Spiced Bean and Mushroom Bowls with Roasted Red Pepper Sauce

My introduction to butter beans happened by pure accident when I picked them up instead of the white beans I actually intended to buy. But what a great mistake it turned out to be! These large, fat beans pack a ton of protein and have a meaty texture that makes them extremely satisfying. I've since been using them regularly to bulk up veggie-heavy meals. Here, they're crisped on the stovetop, tossed with garlic, earthy za'atar, and warm Aleppo pepper, then paired with a medley of sautéed mushrooms for an ultra-hearty, meat-free bowl.

1 Preheat the oven to 400°F (200°C, or gas mark 6).

2 Combine the quinoa, water, and a generous pinch of salt in a medium saucepan. Bring to a boil, then reduce the heat to a simmer and cook, uncovered, until tender, about 15 minutes. Remove from the heat, cover with a lid, and steam for about 5 minutes.

3 Meanwhile, arrange the onion and broccoli on a rimmed baking sheet. Drizzle with 2 tablespoons (30 ml) of the oil, season with salt and pepper, and stir to coat. Roast for 20 minutes, stirring once halfway through.

4 Heat 1 tablespoon (15 ml) oil in a skillet over medium heat. Add the mushrooms, season with salt and pepper, and sauté until browned and tender, about 8 minutes. Stir in the garlic and cook for 2 minutes longer. Transfer the mushrooms to a plate.

5 Heat the remaining 1 tablespoon (15 ml) oil in the same pan. Add the beans, spread in an even layer, and cook until the bottoms are lightly browned, about 3 minutes. Season with za'atar, Aleppo pepper, and salt, and stir to combine. Cook for about 5 minutes longer, until the beans are blistered on all sides.

6 To serve, divide the quinoa among bowls. Top with roasted onion, broccoli, mushrooms, and beans. Drizzle with Roasted Red Pepper Sauce and sprinkle with almonds.

**VEGAN · GLUTEN FREE**

**Serves 4**

1 cup (175 g) quinoa, rinsed
2 cups (470 ml) water
Kosher salt and freshly ground black pepper
1 medium red onion, chopped
1 head broccoli, cut into florets
4 tablespoons (60 ml) avocado or extra-virgin olive oil, divided
4 ounces (115 g) cremini mushrooms, quartered
4 ounces (115 g) shiitake mushrooms, stemmed and sliced
1 clove garlic, minced
3 cups (600 g) or 2 (15-ounce, or 420 g) cans gigante or butter beans, drained and rinsed
2 teaspoons (4 g) za'atar
½ teaspoon Aleppo pepper
1 recipe Roasted Red Pepper Sauce (page 25)
Chopped almonds

# Harvest Macro Bowl

Lately I've been eating macro bowls more than any other type of Buddha bowl. Traditional macro bowls are filled with a combination of whole grains, beans or legumes, tons of vegetables, and some fermented vegetables. They're wholesome and nourishing and, more than anything else, leave me feeling balanced. Here, the brown rice and lentil base lends some meatiness, while the bulk of the bowl is filled with sweet and earthy harvest season veggies, like winter squash, beets, and apple. Sauerkraut finishes the bowl with a tangy bite, plus a dose of probiotics. Try swapping regular sauerkraut for red cabbage or beet kraut.

VEGAN · GLUTEN FREE

**Serves 4**

½ cup (82 g) brown rice
½ cup (96 g) brown lentils
Kosher salt and freshly ground black pepper
1 medium delicata squash
2 tablespoons (30 ml) avocado or extra-virgin olive oil, divided
¼ teaspoon ground cinnamon
1 head broccoli, cut into florets
2 cups (110 g) chopped romaine lettuce
2 medium beets, peeled and thinly sliced
1 large apple, cored and sliced
Sauerkraut
1 recipe Miso Tahini Sauce (page 26)
Hemp seeds

1 Preheat the oven to 400°F (200°C, or gas mark 6).

2 Add the rice, lentils, and a generous pinch of salt to a medium saucepan, and cover with water by at least 2 inches (5 cm). Bring to a boil, then reduce the heat to low and simmer until tender, 25 to 30 minutes. Drain the excess water.

3 Slice the squash into ½-inch (1.3 cm)-thick rings, then remove and discard the seeds. Toss the squash with 1 tablespoon (15 ml) of the oil, cinnamon, salt, and pepper. Arrange in a single layer on one side of a rimmed baking sheet. Toss the broccoli with the remaining 1 tablespoon (15 ml) oil, salt, and pepper, and arrange in a single layer on the other side of the baking sheet. Roast until the vegetables are tender and lightly browned, about 20 minutes, flipping the squash and stirring the broccoli once halfway through.

4 To serve, divide the rice and lentils among bowls. Add the roasted vegetables, romaine, beets, apple, and sauerkraut. Drizzle with Miso Tahini Sauce and sprinkle with hemp seeds.

# Turmeric-Ginger Cauliflower and Lentil Bowls

Between turmeric's warming, bitter, and peppery aroma and its superstar status as a natural anti-inflammatory and antioxidant, it's no wonder I've been reaching for the jar of this spice more and more these days. Here, it's paired with fresh ginger and garlic, and sprinkled over cauliflower rice to create a bowl that feels totally calming, cleansing, and nourishing.

1 Preheat the oven to 425°F (220°C, or gas mark 7).

2 Bring the vinegar, water, and ½ teaspoon of salt to a boil in a medium saucepan, stirring to dissolve the salt. Pour the hot liquid over the sliced onion in a medium bowl; set aside while you prepare the rest of the ingredients.

3 Meanwhile, add the lentils and a generous pinch of salt to a medium saucepan, and cover with water by at least 2 inches (5 cm). Bring to a boil, then reduce the heat to low and simmer until tender, about 25 minutes. Drain the excess water.

4 Toss the sweet potatoes with 1 tablespoon (15 ml) of the oil, salt, and pepper. Arrange in a single layer on a rimmed baking sheet. Roast until tender and browned around the edges, about 20 minutes, stirring once halfway through.

5 Rub the kale with 1 tablespoon (15 ml) oil and a pinch of salt; set aside.

6 Heat the remaining 1 tablespoon (15 ml) oil in a skillet over medium heat. Add the riced cauliflower, ginger, garlic, turmeric, salt, and pepper. Cook, stirring occasionally, until tender, about 3 minutes.

7 Drain the liquid from the onions. To serve, divide the cauliflower rice and lentils among bowls. Top with kale, sweet potato, and pickled onions. Add a generous dollop of Raita and sprinkle with pumpkin seeds.

VEGETARIAN · GLUTEN FREE
**Serves 4**

½ cup (120 ml) white vinegar
½ cup (120 ml) water
Kosher salt and freshly ground black pepper
½ medium red onion, thinly sliced
½ cup (96 g) French lentils, rinsed
2 medium sweet potatoes, peeled and cut into 1-inch (2.5 cm) cubes
3 tablespoons (45 ml) avocado or extra-virgin olive oil, divided
2 cups (140 g) finely shredded Tuscan kale
8 ounces (225 g) riced cauliflower
1 tablespoon (6 g) finely grated fresh ginger
1 clove garlic, minced
1 teaspoon (2 g) ground turmeric
1 recipe Raita (page 25)
Toasted pumpkin seeds

# Sweet Potato and Lentil Taco Bowls

Lentils are one of my favorite picks when it comes to making meatless taco bowls. These tiny pulses pack a punch of protein and have a satisfying meaty texture you just can't get from vegetables alone. Since red lentils don't maintain their firmness very well once cooked, I recommend sticking with the brown lentils called for in the recipe, or even long-cooking French lentils, which both hold their shape well.

VEGETARIAN · GLUTEN FREE

**Serves 4**

1 cup (190 g) brown lentils
Kosher salt and freshly ground black pepper
1 tablespoon (15 ml) avocado or extra-virgin olive oil
16 ounces (455 g) sweet potato noodles
½ teaspoon chili powder
½ teaspoon ground cumin
1 cup (120 g) corn kernels
2 avocados, peeled, pitted, and diced
Greek yogurt
Pico de gallo
2 scallions, thinly sliced
Chopped fresh cilantro

**1** Add the lentils and a generous pinch of salt to a medium saucepan, and cover with water by at least 2 inches (5 cm). Bring to a boil, then reduce the heat to low and simmer until tender, 25 to 30 minutes. Drain the excess water.

**2** Heat the oil in a large skillet over medium heat. Add the sweet potato noodles, chili powder, cumin, salt, and pepper. Cook, tossing occasionally, until soft, 6 to 8 minutes.

**3** To serve, divide the lentils and sweet potato noodles among bowls. Top with corn, avocado, a dollop of Greek yogurt, pico de gallo, scallions, and cilantro.

# Chipotle Sweet Potato Bowls

There are times I'm happy with just a few bites of roasted sweet potato in my bowl, and then there are the times I wish my Buddha bowl were made up of 90 percent sweet potato. This recipe is a delicious tribute to the latter, which I should note does not *actually* make up nearly the entire bowl, but more like half. Thick slices of my favorite orange-hued root vegetable are tossed with chili powder and cumin to balance their natural sweetness, and come out of the oven with a warm, smoky fragrance.

1 Preheat the oven to 400°F (200°C, or gas mark 6).

2 Bring the vinegar, ½ cup (120 ml) of the water, and ½ teaspoon salt to a boil in a small saucepan, stirring to dissolve the salt. Add the onion to a small bowl and pour the hot liquid over the top; set aside.

3 Peel and cut the potatoes in half lengthwise, then cut into ½-inch (1.3 cm)-thick slices. Toss the sweet potatoes with the oil, chipotle chile powder, 1 teaspoon (2 g) of the cumin, salt, and pepper. Spread in an even layer on a rimmed baking sheet. Roast until tender and browned around the edges, about 25 minutes, flipping once halfway through.

4 Meanwhile, combine the quinoa, 2 cups (470 ml) water, and a generous pinch of salt in a medium saucepan. Bring to a boil, then cover, reduce the heat to low, and simmer until tender, about 15 minutes. Remove from the heat, and steam with the lid on for about 5 minutes. Stir in the lime juice.

5 Add the beans, corn, remaining 2 tablespoons (30 ml) water, remaining 1 teaspoon (2 g) cumin, and a pinch of salt to a medium saucepan. Cook, stirring occasionally, until heated through, 3 to 5 minutes.

6 Drain the liquid from the onions. To serve, divide the spinach and quinoa among bowls. Top with sweet potato, black bean–corn mixture, pickled red onions, and avocado. Drizzle with Chimichurri Sauce and sprinkle with scallions.

**VEGAN · GLUTEN FREE**

**Serves 4**

½ cup (120 ml) white vinegar

2½ cups (590 ml) plus 2 tablespoons (30 ml) water, divided

Kosher salt and freshly ground black pepper

½ cup (80 g) thinly sliced red onion

2 large (or 3 medium) sweet potatoes

1 tablespoon (15 ml) avocado or extra-virgin olive oil

1 tablespoon (6 g) chipotle chile powder

2 teaspoons (4 g) ground cumin, divided

1 cup (175 g) quinoa, rinsed

2 tablespoons (30 ml) freshly squeezed lime juice

1½ cups (300 g) or 1 (15-ounce, or 420 g) can black beans, drained and rinsed

1 cup (120 g) corn kernels

4 cups (120 g) baby spinach

1 avocado, peeled, pitted, and thinly sliced

1 recipe Chimichurri Sauce (page 19)

2 scallions, thinly sliced

# Moroccan-Spiced Chickpea Bowls

These saucy, spiced chickpea bowls are all the proof you need that comfort food can also be healthy. Humble chickpeas are the star of the bowl and get transformed by a tomatoey braise, accented with harissa and a medley of cumin, paprika, and cinnamon. Harissa is a North African chili paste that's both smoky and spicy. A little can go a long way, so if you prefer something a little more mild, use about half the amount of harissa called for in the recipe. The bowl is balanced with a pile of sautéed kale and a cool, minty yogurt sauce.

**VEGETARIAN | Serves 4**

3 tablespoons (45 ml) avocado or extra-virgin olive oil, divided
½ medium onion, diced
2 cloves garlic, minced
2 teaspoons (4 g) harissa
1 teaspoon (5 g) tomato paste
2 teaspoons (4 g) ground cumin
1 teaspoon (2 g) paprika
½ teaspoon ground cinnamon
Kosher salt and freshly ground black pepper
2 cups (400 g) chickpeas, drained
1 (14-ounce, or 392 g) can diced tomatoes
¾ cup (125 g) bulgur
1½ cups (355 ml) water
8 packed cups (560 g) shredded kale
2 avocados, peeled, pitted, and thinly sliced
4 poached eggs
1 recipe Mint Yogurt Sauce (page 27)

1 Heat 2 tablespoons (30 ml) of the oil in a skillet over medium heat until shimmering. Add the onion and cook, stirring occasionally, until soft and fragrant, about 5 minutes. Stir in the garlic, harissa, tomato paste, cumin, paprika, cinnamon, salt, and pepper, and cook for 2 minutes. Stir in the chickpeas and tomatoes. Bring to a boil, then reduce the heat to low and simmer for 20 minutes. Meanwhile, prepare the bulgur.

2 Combine the bulgur, water, and a generous pinch of salt in a medium saucepan. Bring to a boil. Reduce the heat to low, cover, and simmer until tender, 10 to 15 minutes.

3 Heat the remaining 1 tablespoon (15 ml) oil in a skillet over medium heat until shimmering. Add the kale and season with salt. Cook, stirring occasionally, until soft and wilted, about 5 minutes.

4 To serve, divide the bulgur among bowls. Top with chickpeas and tomatoes, kale, avocado, and an egg. Drizzle with Mint Yogurt Sauce.

# Winter Squash and Farro Macro Bowls

Of all the varieties of winter squash, delicata is by far my favorite. It's small with an elongated shape, a mild-mannered, not-too-sweet flavor, and covered with a thin, buttery yellow-and-green-striped skin that is totally edible. Yes, unlike butternut and its larger brethren, there is no need to peel delicata squash—you can eat the whole thing, skin and all. For a fun twist, the rings of squash are blanketed with a thin slick of red curry paste. It offsets the sweetness of the vegetable with the subtlest touch of heat and notes of garlic, ginger, and lemongrass. Try this pairing once, and you'll make it again and again.

1 Preheat the oven to 400°F (200°C, or gas mark 6).

2 Add the farro, 2 cups (470 ml) of the water, and a generous pinch of salt to a medium saucepan. Bring to a boil, then reduce the heat to low, cover, and simmer until the farro is tender with a slight chew, about 30 minutes.

3 Add the mung beans, remaining 1½ cups (355 ml) water, and a generous pinch of salt to a separate saucepan. Bring to a boil. Reduce the heat to medium-low and simmer until tender, about 25 minutes. Meanwhile, prepare the vegetables.

4 Whisk together 1 tablespoon (15 ml) of the oil, curry paste, salt, and pepper in a large bowl. Slice the squash in half lengthwise. Scoop out the seeds. Slice crosswise into ½-inch (1.3 cm)-thick crescents. Add the squash to the bowl and toss to combine. Arrange in a single layer on a rimmed baking sheet, and roast until tender and browned around the edges, 25 minutes, flipping once halfway through.

5 Heat the remaining 1 tablespoon (15 ml) oil in a large skillet over medium heat. Add the chard, ginger, and salt. Cook, tossing occasionally, until wilted, about 5 minutes.

6 To serve, divide the farro among bowls. Top with mung beans, roasted squash, chard, beets, goat cheese, pumpkin seeds, and pesto.

**VEGETARIAN** | **Serves 4**

1 cup (165 g) pearled farro
3½ cups (822 ml) water, divided
Kosher salt and freshly ground black pepper
½ cup (25 g) dried mung beans, rinsed
2 tablespoons (30 ml) avocado or extra-virgin olive oil, divided
½ tablespoon (7 g) vegetarian Thai red curry paste
2 medium delicata squash
1 bunch rainbow chard, shredded
½ tablespoon (3 g) grated fresh ginger
2 medium beets, peeled and thinly sliced
Crumbled goat cheese
Toasted pumpkin seeds
1 recipe Cilantro-Parsley Pesto (page 21)

# Beet Falafel Bowls

If you eat falafel bowls as much as I do, I'm certain you understand the need to shake things up once in a while. Here, oven-baked falafel patties are jazzed up with jewel-toned beet noodles, roasted vegetables, and a tangy, herb-packed avocado sauce. If you're making the spiralized beet noodles at home, three or four medium beets should be just enough.

**VEGETARIAN | Serves 4**

- 3 cups (600 g) or 2 (15-ounce, or 420 g) cans chickpeas, drained and rinsed
- 1 small red onion, roughly chopped
- ½ packed cup (24 g) fresh parsley leaves
- ½ packed cup (24 g) fresh cilantro leaves
- 2 tablespoons (30 ml) freshly squeezed lemon juice
- 2 cloves garlic
- 2 teaspoons (4 g) ground cumin
- 1 teaspoon (2 g) ground coriander
- ⅛ teaspoon cayenne pepper
- Kosher salt and freshly ground black pepper
- 3 tablespoons (24 g) all-purpose flour
- 1 teaspoon (2 g) baking powder
- 8 (5-inch, or 13 cm) baby carrots, with stems still attached
- 1 tablespoon (15 ml) avocado or extra-virgin olive oil
- 16 ounces (455 g) spiralized beet noodles
- 2 packed cups (140 g) finely shredded Tuscan kale
- ½ English cucumber, chopped
- 1 recipe Avocado Green Goddess Dressing (page 16)

1 If using dried beans, add the chickpeas to a medium bowl and cover with water by at least 1 inch (2.5 cm). Let them sit, uncovered, at room temperature for 24 hours.

2 Preheat the oven to 375°F (190°C, or gas mark 5).

3 Add the drained chickpeas, onion, parsley, cilantro, lemon juice, garlic, cumin, coriander, cayenne, 1 teaspoon (6 g) salt, and ¼ teaspoon pepper to the bowl of a food processor. Pulse about 10 times until the chickpeas are chopped. Scrape down the sides of the bowl, add the flour and baking powder, and pulse until the mixture is well combined.

4 Scoop out about 2 tablespoons (30 g) of the mixture and roll it into a ball in the palms of your hands. Transfer to a lightly greased baking sheet and use a spatula to flatten into a ½-inch (1.3 cm)-thick disk. Repeat with the remainder of the mixture.

5 Bake the falafel until cooked through and tender, 25 to 30 minutes, flipping once halfway through.

6 Cut the carrots in half lengthwise. Toss with the oil, salt, and pepper, and arrange in a single layer on a rimmed baking sheet. Cook until tender, about 20 minutes.

7 To serve, divide the beet noodles and kale among bowls. Top with falafel patties, roasted carrots, and cucumber, and drizzle with Avocado Green Goddess Dressing.

**Make It Gluten-Free** | Make the falafel patties gluten free by using an equal amount of all-purpose gluten-free flour, almond meal, or chickpea flour.

# Ethiopian-Spiced Red Lentil Bowls with Greens

Berbere is a classic, all-purpose spice blend used in Ethiopian cooking, from slow-simmered stews to meat, vegetables, and lentils. While recipes vary, this fiery red mixture typically combines fenugreek, cardamom, cumin, chiles, ginger, paprika, and more. Berbere has a warm, spiced aroma, with a balance of sweet, spicy, and bitter flavors.

**VEGETARIAN · GLUTEN FREE**

**Serves 4**

¾ cup (125 g) brown rice
1½ cups (355 ml) water
Kosher salt and freshly ground black pepper
2 bunches broccolini
3 tablespoons (45 ml) avocado or extra-virgin olive oil, divided
1 onion, diced
2 cloves garlic, minced
1 tablespoon (6 g) finely grated fresh ginger
2 tablespoons (30 g) tomato paste
1 tablespoon (6 g) berbere
1 teaspoon (2 g) ground coriander
1 cup (190 g) red lentils
4 cups (940 ml) vegetable or chicken broth
1 cup (235 ml) canned unsweetened coconut milk
4 cups (120 g) baby spinach
Greek yogurt
Fresh cilantro leaves

1 Preheat the oven to 400°F (200°C, or gas mark 6).

2 Add the rice, water, and a generous pinch of salt to a medium saucepan and bring to a boil. Reduce the heat to low, cover, and cook until the rice is tender, 40 to 45 minutes. Remove from the heat, and steam the rice with the lid on for 10 minutes.

3 Toss the broccolini with 2 tablespoons (30 ml) of the oil, salt, and pepper. Arrange in a single layer on a rimmed baking sheet. Roast until tender and the florets are lightly browned, about 15 minutes, stirring once halfway through.

4 Meanwhile, heat the remaining 1 tablespoon (15 ml) oil in a large skillet over medium heat. Add the onion and cook, stirring occasionally, until soft, about 5 minutes. Stir in the garlic, ginger, tomato paste, berbere, coriander, salt, and pepper, and cook 1 to 2 minutes longer. Add the lentils, broth, and coconut milk, and stir to combine. Bring to a boil, then reduce the heat and simmer, stirring occasionally, until soft, 20 to 25 minutes.

5 To serve, divide the spinach and rice among bowls. Top with lentils, roasted broccolini, yogurt, and cilantro.

# Turmeric-Roasted Vegetable Bowls

Turns out there is a way to make roasted vegetables even better than they already are. Yes, really, it's true. Sprinkle this mix of crunchy cauliflower, carrots, and beets with a duo of ground turmeric and cumin, and not only do you get the charred edges that make roasted veggies so great, but they also have a warm, smoky aroma that tastes seriously nourishing. On its own, turmeric has pungent, bitter undertones, but this bowl keeps them in check with a mix of sweet root vegetables, a runny-yolked egg, and a creamy Cilantro Yogurt Sauce.

1 Preheat the oven to 400°F (200°C, or gas mark 6).

2 Toss the cauliflower, carrots, and beets with 2 tablespoons (30 ml) of the oil, turmeric, cumin, salt, and pepper. Arrange the vegetables in an even layer on a rimmed baking sheet. Roast until tender and browned around the edges, about 20 minutes, stirring once halfway through.

3 Meanwhile, heat 1 tablespoon (15 ml) oil in a medium saucepan. Add the millet, stir to coat, and toast until golden brown, 4 to 5 minutes. Pour in 1½ cups (355 ml) of the water and a pinch of salt. The water will bubble and spurt at first, but will settle quickly. Bring to a boil, then reduce the heat to low, cover, and simmer until tender, about 15 minutes. Remove from the heat and steam in the pot for 5 minutes.

4 Heat the remaining 1 tablespoon (15 ml) oil in a large skillet over medium heat. Add the kale, salt, and red pepper flakes. Cook, stirring occasionally, until just wilted. Pour in the remaining ¼ cup (60 ml) water and cook until the greens are soft and the liquid is absorbed, about 5 minutes.

5 To serve, divide the millet among bowls. Top with roasted vegetables, kale, a poached egg, radishes, and scallions. Drizzle with Cilantro Yogurt Sauce and garnish with sprouts.

**VEGETARIAN · GLUTEN FREE**

**Serves 4**

½ head medium cauliflower, cut into florets

½ pound (224 g) baby carrots, leafy tops removed

4 medium beets, trimmed, peeled, and diced

4 tablespoons (60 ml) avocado or extra-virgin olive oil, divided

1 teaspoon (2 g) ground turmeric

1 teaspoon (2 g) ground cumin

Kosher salt and freshly ground black pepper

¾ cup (130 g) millet

1¾ cups (410 ml) water, divided

4 packed cups (280 g) shredded kale

⅛ teaspoon red pepper flakes

4 poached eggs

8 radishes, trimmed and quartered

2 scallions, green parts only, thinly sliced

1 recipe Cilantro Yogurt Sauce (page 27)

Broccoli, clover, or alfalfa sprouts

# Chili-Lime Portobello Bowls

Is it just me, or are there not nearly enough dinner recipes that put enormous portobello mushrooms front and center? I'm certain it's not just me. Let's make a vow to remedy that by putting these taco-inspired bowls into your dinner rotation. Cut into thick strips, coated with a smoky, spiced seasoning, and cooked until tender, portobello mushrooms bring an ultra-satisfying meatiness to this meal.

If you're a weekend meal prepper, like me, you'll appreciate that all of the components for this bowl can be made in advance. In fact, the corn salsa is even better on the second and third day. When dinner rolls around, reheat the rice and mushrooms, or assemble the bowls and enjoy chilled.

**VEGAN · GLUTEN FREE**

**Serves 4**

1 cup (165 g) brown rice
2 cups (470 ml) water
Kosher salt and freshly ground black pepper
4 large portobello mushroom caps
2 tablespoons (30 ml) avocado or extra-virgin olive oil
1 teaspoon (2 g) chili powder
1 teaspoon (2 g) ground cumin
1½ cups (180 g) corn kernels
½ cup (80 g) diced red onion
1 jalapeño, seeded and diced
¼ cup (4 g) finely chopped cilantro
Juice of 1 lime
2 cups (140 g) shredded red cabbage
1 cup (150 g) cherry tomatoes, halved
1 recipe Avocado Sauce (page 17)

1 Preheat the oven to 400°F (200°C, or gas mark 6).

2 Add the rice, water, and a generous pinch of salt to a medium saucepan and bring to a boil. Reduce the heat to low, cover, and cook until the rice is tender, about 40 minutes. Remove from the heat and steam the rice with the lid on for 10 minutes.

3 Slice the mushrooms in half, then cut into ½-inch (1.3 cm)-thick slices. Toss gently with the oil, chili powder, cumin, salt, and pepper until the mushrooms are well coated. Spread in an even layer on a rimmed baking sheet. Roast until the mushrooms are soft and cooked through, about 12 minutes.

4 Add the corn, red onion, jalapeño, cilantro, and lime juice to small bowl, and stir to combine.

5 To serve, divide the rice among bowls. Top with mushrooms, corn salsa, cabbage, and tomatoes, then drizzle with Avocado Sauce.

# Fruit
# BOWLS

Summer Fruit Salad Bowls  **158**

Strawberry Banana Nice Cream Bowls  **159**

Pumpkin Pie Cheesecake Bowls  **160**

Winter Fruit Salad Bowls  **161**

Creamy Freekeh Bowls with
Honey-Balsamic Stewed Strawberries  **162**

Ricotta and Honey Roasted Plum Bowls
with Crunchy Buckwheat  **165**

Lime-Avocado Pudding Bowls  **166**

Chamomile Poached Pear Bowls  **167**

Chocolate-Tahini Chia Pudding Bowls  **168**

Coconut Chia and Tropical Fruit Bowls  **169**

# Summer Fruit Salad Bowls

This is not just another fruit salad. It's your solution for showing off summer's finest with sweet sophistication and the kind of simplicity the season begs for. It's finished with a lightly infused simple syrup that perfumes the fruit with the delicate hint of rose and vanilla. You'll wonder why you haven't been adding it to your fruit bowls all along.

VEGAN | **Serves 4**

3 tablespoons (36 g) sugar
1 cup (235 ml) and 3 tablespoons (45 ml) water, divided
1 vanilla bean, split and seeds scraped out
¾ teaspoon rose water
½ cup (80 g) bulgur
Fine sea salt
1 large ripe peach, pitted and thinly sliced
1 cup cherries, pitted and halved
8 strawberries, hulled and quartered
1 cup (145 g) blackberries
Chopped fresh mint

1 Combine the sugar, 3 tablespoons (45 ml) of the water, vanilla bean and seeds, and rose water in a small saucepan over medium-high heat. Bring to a boil, whisking until the sugar dissolves. Remove from the heat and steep for 20 minutes.

2 Meanwhile, combine the bulgur, remaining 1 cup (235 ml) water, and a generous pinch of salt in a medium saucepan. Bring to a boil, then cover, reduce the heat to low, and simmer until tender, 10 to 15 minutes.

3 Remove and discard the vanilla bean from the syrup. To serve, divide the bulgur among bowls. Arrange the fruit around the top of the bowl, then drizzle with vanilla-rose syrup and sprinkle with mint.

# Strawberry Banana Nice Cream Bowls

Don't be surprised if you're halfway through this bowl and you forget that you're not eating actual ice cream. It happens to me almost every time, and that's saying a lot as someone who *loves*—and I mean *really* loves—ice cream. Mixed with frozen strawberries and bananas, a splash of cashew milk, and a couple of special ingredients to give this popular pairing a twist, it hits your bowl with the consistency of soft-serve and a faint hint of flakiness that just might remind you of sorbet.

I've tried several methods for making nice cream, and time and again my high-speed blender leaves me with the smoothest, most evenly blended results. However, don't be deterred if you're working with a regular blender or food processor, as both will still get the job done.

1 Add the frozen bananas to a high-speed blender. Process continuously until the bananas are broken down into small crumbles. Scrape down the sides of the jar, if necessary, and add the frozen strawberries, cashew milk, vanilla, ginger, and salt. Continue processing on high speed until smooth and creamy, using the tamper to push the ingredients down, as necessary.

2 To serve, divide among bowls immediately. Top with fresh strawberries, fresh bananas, granola, and coconut flakes.

**VEGAN**

**Serves 4**

4 frozen peeled bananas, cut into chunks
2 cups (290 g) frozen strawberries
1 cup (235 ml) unsweetened cashew milk
1 teaspoon (5 ml) vanilla extract
½ teaspoon ground ginger
¼ teaspoon fine sea salt
Sliced fresh strawberries
Sliced fresh bananas
Granola
Unsweetened coconut flakes

# Pumpkin Pie Cheesecake Bowls

This bowl was created as my answer to a spiced pumpkin dessert that's a bit more wholesome than the seasonal custard pie, yet still with just enough full-flavored richness to make it feel like a real treat. And boy, does it deliver. A duo of cream cheese and Greek yogurt gives this lush whipped pumpkin body and richness, and the most wonderful tang that will remind you of cheesecake.

**VEGETARIAN**

**Serves 4**

4 ounces (115 g) cream cheese, softened
1 cup (240 g) plain Greek yogurt, plus more for topping
1 cup (260 g) pumpkin puree
¼ cup (60 ml) maple syrup
1 teaspoon (5 ml) vanilla extract
2 teaspoons (4 g) ground cinnamon
1 teaspoon (2 g) ground ginger
½ teaspoon ground nutmeg
Fine sea salt
1 cup (150 g) granola
Toasted pumpkin seeds
Chopped pecans
Pomegranate arils
Cacao nibs

1 Add the cream cheese, yogurt, pumpkin puree, maple syrup, vanilla, spices, and a pinch of salt to the bowl of a food processor or blender, and process until smooth and creamy. Transfer to a bowl, cover, and chill in the refrigerator for at least 4 hours.

2 To serve, divide the granola among dessert bowls. Top with the pumpkin mixture, a dollop of Greek yogurt, pumpkin seeds, pecans, pomegranate arils, and cacao nibs.

# Winter Fruit Salad Bowls

Do not discount the winter months when it comes to fresh fruit! And know that there are more than work-a-day navel oranges to be had. I created this bowl to show off the bright colors and varied textures of the most vibrant winter fruits. But what really makes it sing is the warm ginger–vanilla bean syrup that gets drizzled over the top right before serving. It's a simple dessert bowl, with components that can be prepped in advance, and beautiful enough to serve for guests.

1 Add the farro, 1¼ cups (295 ml) of the water, and a generous pinch of salt to a medium saucepan. Bring to a boil, then reduce the heat to low, cover, and simmer until the farro is tender with a slight chew, about 30 minutes.

2 Combine the sugar, remaining 3 tablespoons (45 ml) water, vanilla bean and seeds, and ginger in a small saucepan over medium-high heat. Bring to a boil, whisking until the sugar dissolves. Remove from the heat and steep for 20 minutes. Meanwhile, prepare the fruit.

3 Slice off the ends of the grapefruit. Set on a flat work surface, cut-side down. Use a sharp knife to cut away the peel and white pith, following the curve of the fruit, from top to bottom. Cut between the membranes to remove the segments of the fruit. Repeat the same process to peel and segment the blood orange.

4 Remove and discard the ginger and vanilla bean from the syrup. To serve, divide the farro among bowls. Arrange the fruit around the top of the bowl, sprinkle with pomegranate arils, and then drizzle with ginger-vanilla syrup.

VEGAN | **Serves 4**

½ cup (80 g) pearled farro
1¼ cups (295 ml) plus 3 tablespoons (45 ml) water, divided
Fine sea salt
3 tablespoons (36 g) sugar
1 vanilla bean, split and seeds scraped out
1-inch (2.5 cm) piece fresh ginger, thinly sliced
1 large pink grapefruit
1 blood orange
1 persimmon, thinly sliced
1 Asian pear, cored and thinly sliced
1 cup (120 g) pomegranate arils

# Creamy Freekeh Bowls with Honey-Balsamic Stewed Strawberries

One thing you should know about me is that I am a firm believer in dessert. Always. I'm particularly fond of recipes that can be pulled together at a moment's notice, and are quick enough to make on a weeknight. This creamy bowl with a sweet and tangy fruit topping is one of my favorites, and hits the spot every time. When I want to make it taste a touch richer, I like stirring a splash of cream into the freekeh once it comes off the stove, though this is totally optional. And whether you choose to serve it warm right on the spot or make the whole thing in advance and serve it chilled, you can't go wrong either way.

VEGETARIAN | **Serves 4**

⅓ cup (55 g) cracked freekeh
1¼ cups (295 ml) milk (dairy or nondairy)
Fine sea salt
1 teaspoon (5 ml) vanilla extract
½ teaspoon ground cinnamon
¼ cup (60 ml) heavy cream (optional)
1 quart (580 g) strawberries, hulled and roughly chopped
2 tablespoons (40 g) honey
1 tablespoon (15 ml) balsamic vinegar
2 cups (480 g) vanilla yogurt
Chopped pistachios
Hemp seeds

1 Add the freekeh, milk, and a pinch of salt to a medium saucepan and stir to combine. Bring to a boil, then reduce the heat to low, cover, and simmer for 15 to 20 minutes, stirring occasionally, until tender. Remove from the heat and stir in the vanilla, cinnamon, and cream (if desired).

2 Meanwhile, combine the strawberries, honey, balsamic vinegar, and a pinch of salt in a separate saucepan and bring to a boil. Reduce the heat to low, and cook, uncovered, stirring occasionally, until the juices are syrupy and the berries are soft, about 10 minutes. Remove from the heat.

3 To serve, divide the freekeh among bowls. Spoon the stewed berries over the top, add a dollop of yogurt, and sprinkle with pistachios and hemp seeds.

# Ricotta and Honey Roasted Plum Bowls with Crunchy Buckwheat

After I joined a farm share last summer, there were many weeks I found myself with more plums than I knew what to do with. I couldn't eat them fast enough. So, I started roasting them with a drizzle of olive oil and honey. It proved an easy way to use a bunch of these sweet stone fruits at once, and an especially great use for plums that are on their last legs. The heat of the oven concentrates the natural sugars in the fruit, while the honey imparts subtle floral notes. I encourage you to pick up some good-quality ricotta for this sweet and savory treat—it's worth it.

1 Preheat the oven to 425°F (220°C, or gas mark 7).

2 Place the plums cut-side up on a rimmed baking sheet. Brush with 1 tablespoon (15 ml) of the olive oil and drizzle with the honey. Roast until tender and lightly caramelized, about 15 minutes.

3 Meanwhile, heat the remaining 1 tablespoon (15 ml) oil in a skillet over medium heat until shimmering. Add the buckwheat and cook, stirring frequently, until the buckwheat is crispy and toasted, 5 to 8 minutes. If it starts to brown too quickly or burn, lower the heat.

4 To serve, divide the ricotta among bowls. Top with roasted plums, crispy buckwheat, and walnuts. Garnish with an extra drizzle of honey and olive oil and a pinch of Maldon salt, if desired.

VEGETARIAN | **Serves 4**

4 plums, halved and pitted
2 tablespoons (30 ml) extra-virgin olive oil, divided, plus more for drizzling
2 tablespoons (40 g) honey, plus more for drizzling
¼ cup (40 g) kasha buckwheat
2 cups (480 g) ricotta
Chopped walnuts
Maldon sea salt (optional)

# Lime-Avocado Pudding Bowls

I always love when I stumble on a recipe that teaches me to experience a food in a brand-new light. That's exactly what these pudding bowls do with avocado. In fact, when you taste this lush pudding, you'd never guess that avocado is the main ingredient. It will get your taste buds firing on all cylinders with its bold lime flavor that's just the right balance of sweet, tart, and tangy. By all accounts this is a light dessert, though the fattiness of the avocado adds a lovely richness and makes it filling.

VEGETARIAN · GLUTEN FREE

**Serves 4**

3 ripe avocados, peeled and pitted
½ cup (120 g) plain Greek yogurt
½ cup (120 ml) freshly squeezed lime juice
2 tablespoons (30 ml) freshly squeezed lemon juice
Zest from 1 lime
4 tablespoons (80 g) honey or agave syrup
½ teaspoon vanilla extract
Fine sea salt
Unsweetened toasted coconut flakes
Chopped cashews
Kiwi, peeled and sliced
Raspberries

1 Add the avocado flesh, yogurt, lime juice, lemon juice, lime zest, honey or agave, vanilla, and pinch of salt to the bowl of a food processor. Process continuously until well combined and smooth, about 1 minute.

2 Divide the pudding among bowls. Top with coconut flakes, cashews, kiwi, and raspberries.

**Make It Vegan** | It's incredibly easy to adapt this dessert bowl to be vegan-friendly. Stick with agave as the sweetener and swap the Greek yogurt for a nondairy yogurt. Cashew and almond yogurts are my top picks for a substitute, though coconut and soy yogurts also work nicely.

# Chamomile Poached Pear Bowls

This is the bowl I make anytime I want to feel like a total dessert wizard. Poached pears are wildly impressive and elegant, yet they could not be easier to make. Simmered in lightly sweetened chamomile tea, the pears are infused with a delicate floral aroma and then partnered with super earthy amaranth and orange blossom–scented yogurt.

Bosc pears, which I call for in the recipe, are a great choice for poaching, because they hold their shape well when cooked.

1 Combine the amaranth, 1½ cups (355 ml) of the water, and a pinch of salt in a medium saucepan. Bring to a boil, then reduce the heat to low, cover, and simmer until tender and the water is mostly absorbed, 25 to 30 minutes. Stir occasionally to prevent the amaranth from sticking to the bottom of the pan. Remove from the heat and stir in the milk and cinnamon.

2 Bring the remaining 4 cups (940 ml) water to a boil in a large saucepan. Remove from the heat, add the tea bags and 3 table-spoons (60 g) of the honey, and stir until the honey is dissolved. Steep for 5 minutes. Remove and discard the tea bags. Return the pan to the heat and bring the liquid to a simmer. Reduce the heat to low, add the pears, cover, and cook until the pears are tender, 15 to 20 minutes.

3 Meanwhile, stir together the yogurt, remaining 1 tablespoon (20 g) honey, and orange blossom water in a small bowl.

4 To serve, divide the amaranth among bowls. Top with pears, yogurt, and shaved chocolate.

VEGETARIAN · GLUTEN FREE

**Serves 4**

½ cup (80 g) amaranth
5½ cups (1293 ml) water, divided
Fine sea salt
½ cup (120 ml) milk
¼ teaspoon ground cinnamon
4 chamomile tea bags
4 tablespoons (80 g) honey, divided
4 Bosc pears, peeled, halved
   lengthwise, and cored
½ cup (120 g) plain yogurt
1 teaspoon (5 ml) orange blossom
   water
Shaved chocolate

# Chocolate-Tahini Chia Pudding Bowls

If the magical duo of chocolate and peanut butter makes you swoon, I am certain you are going to love this dessert. Made from sesame seeds, tahini has a rich, creamy texture and a nutty flavor, with a touch more earthiness than peanut butter. It is also a wonderful complement to all things chocolate, which here comes in the form of cocoa powder. A spoonful of tahini balances the richness of the cocoa and sweetness of the dates, adding an extra, unexpected layer of depth to your dessert bowl.

VEGAN · GLUTEN FREE

**Serves 4**

2½ cups (590 ml) almond, cashew, or coconut milk
6 pitted dates
3 tablespoons (24 g) unsweetened natural cocoa powder
1 tablespoon (15 g) tahini
1 teaspoon (5 ml) vanilla extract
¼ teaspoon ground cinnamon
¼ teaspoon fine sea salt
½ cup (48 g) chia seeds
¼ cup (15 g) whipped cream
Cacao nibs
Pomegranate arils
Sesame seeds

1 Add the milk, dates, cocoa powder, tahini, vanilla, cinnamon, and salt to a blender, and blend on high speed until the dates are totally broken down and the liquid is smooth. Add the chia seeds and blend just until combined. Pour into a large bowl, cover, and refrigerate for at least 6 hours or overnight.

2 To serve, divide the chia pudding among bowls. Top with whipped cream, cacao nibs, pomegranate arils, and sesame seeds.

# Coconut Chia and Tropical Fruit Bowls

One of the things I love most about traveling anywhere tropical (well, after the white sand, turquoise waters, and sunshine, of course) is the bounty of lush fruits. So adding them to this dessert bowl instantly makes it feel special. The sweetness of the mango and pineapple, plus the sweet-tart bite of the passion fruit, also work well to balance the richness of the coconut milk.

1 Whisk together the milks, coconut yogurt, agave, cinnamon, nutmeg, and salt in a large bowl or wide-mouth jar. Add the chia seeds and whisk until evenly dispersed.

2 Cover and refrigerate for at least 6 hours or overnight to thicken the pudding.

3 To serve, divide the chia pudding among bowls. Top with passion fruit, mango, star fruit, pineapple, and coconut flakes.

VEGAN · GLUTEN FREE

**Serves 4**

1 (14-ounce, or 392 g) can unsweetened coconut milk

1 cup (235 ml) unsweetened almond milk

1 cup (240 g) coconut yogurt

3 tablespoons (45 ml) agave syrup

½ teaspoon ground cinnamon

¼ teaspoon ground nutmeg

¼ teaspoon fine sea salt

¾ cup (72 g) chia seeds

1 passion fruit

1 mango, peeled, pitted, and cubed

1 star fruit, thinly sliced

1 cup (165 g) diced pineapple

Unsweetened coconut flakes

## ACKNOWLEDGMENTS

To my editor Dan Rosenberg and the entire team at Harvard Common Press and The Quarto Group: Thank you for coaching me along, showing me that I'm capable of big things in a short amount of time, and, most of all, for bringing this project to life.

Maria Siriano: You are truly a wonder woman. Many thanks for capturing my vision so beautifully and taking on this project during what was certainly such a crazy time.

Thank you also to Karen Levy for having an impeccable eye for detail.

Faith Durand: I am forever grateful that you took a chance and brought me onto the Kitchn team, and for thinking of me and planting the seed for this project.

The Kitchn team: You all constantly inspire me and make me a better writer and person.

My family and friends: Your endless support, love, encouragement, and willingness to taste and test my recipes means the world to me. I could not have done this without you.

And finally, the most heartfelt thank you to my husband, Lucien. You have been my dishwasher, taste tester, and number one supporter every step of the way. Thank you for always believing in me and pushing me to follow my dreams.

## ABOUT THE AUTHOR

**Kelli Foster** is a recipe developer and food editor at the popular cooking site Kitchn and author of *Everyday Freekeh Meals*. Her work has also been featured on Greatist and the *Dr. Oz Show*. She lives in New York City.

# INDEX

## A

Ahi tuna
  Sesame Tuna Bowls, 66
Almonds, unsalted
  Almond-Quinoa and Salmon Bowls, 57
  Roasted Red Pepper Sauce, 25
Apples
  Apple Pie Farro Breakfast Bowls, 31
  Butternut Squash and Kale Bowls, 126
  Harvest Macro Bowl, 142
  Pomegranate and Freekeh Breakfast
    Tabbouleh Bowls, 35
Arugula
  Almond-Quinoa and Salmon Bowls, 57
  Cauliflower Falafel Power Bowls, 124
  Dukkah-Crusted Chicken and Barley
    Bowls, 82
  Herbed Chickpea and Bulgur Bowls, 125
  Lamb Meatball Bowls with Sweet Potato
    Noodles and Green Tahini, 110
  Lentil and Smoked Salmon Niçoise
    Bowls, 56
  Moroccan Salmon and Millet Bowls, 61
  Summertime Green Goddess Steak
    Bowls, 99
  Warm Autumn Chicken and Wild Rice
    Bowls, 85
Asparagus
  Brown Rice and Kale Pesto Bowls, 122
  Crispy White Bean and Pesto Bowls, 117
  Green Goddess Quinoa Bowls with Crispy
    Tofu, 119
  Spring Soba Bowls, 133

## B

Balsamic Shrimp and Farro Bowls, 72
Bananas
  Strawberry Banana Nice Cream Bowls, 159
Banh Mi Bowls, 128
Basic Everyday Vinaigrette, 18
Basil, fresh
  Avocado Green Goddess Dressing, 16
  Beef and Broccoli Bowls, 100
  Peachy Basil Chicken and Rice Bowls, 88
  Vietnamese Zucchini Noodle and Shrimp
    Bowls, 70
BBQ Chicken Quinoa Bowls, 86
Bean sprouts
  Cauliflower Pad Thai Bowls, 135
Beans
  Black Bean and Chorizo Bowls, 46

Buckwheat and Black Bean Breakfast
  Bowls, 48
Chipotle Sweet Potato Bowls, 145
Crispy White Bean and Pesto Bowls, 117
Quinoa and Chicken Taco Bowls with
  Cilantro-Lime Dressing, 80
Spiced Bean and Mushroom Bowls with
  Roasted Red Pepper Sauce, 141
Steak Fajita Spaghetti Squash Bowls, 98
Tomato-Braised Cod and Barley Bowls, 65
Winter Chili Bowls with Beef, Beans, and
  Greens, 106
Beef
  Beef and Broccoli Bowls, 100
  Ginger Beef Bowls, 105
  Korean-Style Beef Bowls with Zucchini
    Noodles, 10
  Miso Noodle Bowls with Stir-Fried Beef, 103
  Steak Fajita Spaghetti Squash Bowls, 98
  Summertime Green Goddess Steak
    Bowls, 99
  Winter Chili Bowls with Beef, Beans, and
    Greens, 106
Beets
  Almond-Quinoa and Salmon Bowls, 57
  Beet Falafel Bowls, 150
  Chicken Kofta Bowls, 92
  Harvest Macro Bowl, 142
  Herbed Chicken and Root Vegetable
    Bowls, 93
  Lentil Quinoa Bowls with Harissa Lamb
    Meatballs, 111
  Smoky Lemon Brussels Sprout Bowls with
    Turkey Meatballs, 94
  Superfood Salmon Bowls, 74
  Turmeric-Roasted Vegetable Bowls, 153
  Winter Squash and Farro Macro Bowls, 149
  Za'atar Chickpea Bowls, 120
Bell peppers
  Balsamic Shrimp and Farro Bowls, 72
  Cauliflower Falafel Power Bowls, 124
  Green Curry Chicken and Quinoa
    Bowls, 79
  Quinoa and Chicken Taco Bowls with
    Cilantro-Lime Dressing, 80
  Scrambled Chickpea Breakfast Bowls, 49
  Spicy Thai Chicken and Brown Rice
    Bowls, 89
  Steak Fajita Spaghetti Squash Bowls, 98

Bittersweet Citrus and Salmon Power
  Bowls, 62
Blackberries
  Blackberry Millet Breakfast Bowls, 32
  Summer Fruit Salad Bowls, 158
Bok choy
  Beef and Broccoli Bowls, 100
  Ginger Beef Bowls, 105
  Ginger Peanut Soba Noodle Bowls, 78
  Sesame Tuna Bowls, 66
Bowls, choosing, 10
Broccoli
  Beef and Broccoli Bowls, 100
  Broccoli Rice and Egg Bowls, 134
  Green Goddess Quinoa Bowls with Crispy
    Tofu, 119
  Harvest Macro Bowl, 142
  Herbed Chickpea and Bulgur Bowls, 125
  Lentil and Roasted Tomatillo Bowls, 127
  Lentil Quinoa Bowls with Harissa Lamb
    Meatballs, 111
  making riced, 12
  Spiced Bean and Mushroom Bowls with
    Roasted Red Pepper Sauce, 141
  Spicy Sesame Tofu and Rice Bowls, 136
  Super Green Quinoa Bowls, 116
  Thai Coconut Curry Bowls, 131
  Tomato-Braised Cod and Barley Bowls, 65
Broccolini
  Almond-Quinoa and Salmon Bowls, 57
  Ethiopian-Spiced Red Lentil Bowls with
    Greens, 152
  Turkey and Cabbage Stir-Fry Bowls with
    Almond Butter Sauce, 95
Brown Rice and Kale Pesto Bowls, 122
Brown Rice Bowls with Seared Fish and
  Chimichurri, 75
Brussels sprouts
  Bittersweet Citrus and Salmon Power
    Bowls, 62
  Butternut Squash and Kale Bowls, 126
  Smoky Lemon Brussels Sprout Bowls with
    Turkey Meatballs, 94
  Tofu Scramble Bowls with Kale and Brussels
    Sprouts, 52
  Warm Autumn Chicken and Wild Rice
    Bowls, 85
Buckwheat and Black Bean Breakfast
  Bowls, 48
Butternut Squash and Kale Bowls, 126

**C**

Cabbage, red
    Cauliflower Pad Thai Bowls, 135
    Chili-Maple Tofu Bowls, 139
    Chili-Lime Portobello Bowls, 154
    Chimichurri Chicken Bowls, 87
    Green Curry Chicken and Quinoa
        Bowls, 79
    Herbed Chickpea and Bulgur Bowls, 125
    Miso Noodle Bowls with Stir-Fried
        Beef, 103
    Quinoa and Chicken Taco Bowls with
        Cilantro-Lime Dressing, 80
    Spicy Thai Chicken and Brown Rice
        Bowls, 89
    Steak Fajita Spaghetti Squash Bowls, 98
    Thai Coconut Curry Bowls, 131
    Turkey and Cabbage Stir-Fry Bowls with
        Almond Butter Sauce, 95
Carrots
    Banh Mi Bowls, 128
    Beet Falafel Bowls, 150
    Brown Rice Bowls with Seared Fish and
        Chimichurri, 75
    Cauliflower Pad Thai Bowls, 135
    Chili-Maple Tofu Bowls, 139
    Ginger Peanut Soba Noodle Bowls, 78
    Herbed Chicken and Root Vegetable
        Bowls, 93
    Korean-Style Beef Bowls with Zucchini
        Noodles, 102
    Masala Chickpea Bowls, 140
    Miso Noodle Bowls with Stir-Fried
        Beef, 103
    Moroccan Salmon and Millet Bowls, 61
    Shrimp Summer Roll Bowls, 69
    Spicy Sesame Tofu and Rice Bowls, 136
    Spicy Thai Chicken and Brown Rice
        Bowls, 89
    Spring Soba Bowls, 133
    Turmeric-Roasted Vegetable Bowls, 153
    Vegetarian Sushi Bowls, 132
    Vietnamese Zucchini Noodle and Shrimp
        Bowls, 70
    Za'atar Chickpea Bowls, 120
Cauliflower
    Black Bean and Chorizo Bowls, 46
    Brown Rice and Kale Pesto Bowls, 122
    Cauliflower Falafel Power Bowls, 124
    Cauliflower Pad Thai Bowls, 135
    Cauliflower Tabbouleh Bowls with Lamb
        Meatballs, 112
    Lamb and Roasted Cauliflower Taco Bowls
        with Chimichurri, 113

    making riced, 12
    Masala Chickpea Bowls, 140
    Scrambled Chickpea Breakfast Bowls, 49
    Turmeric-Ginger Cauliflower and Lentil
        Bowls, 143
    Turmeric-Roasted Vegetable Bowls, 153
Chai-Spiced Multigrain Porridge Bowls, 38
Chamomile Poached Pear Bowls, 167
Chard
    Green Curry Chicken and Quinoa
        Bowls, 79
    Harissa Chicken Bowls, 83
    Lentil Quinoa Bowls with Harissa Lamb
        Meatballs, 111
    Masala Chickpea Bowls, 140
    Winter Squash and Farro Macro
        Bowls, 149
Cherries
    Summer Fruit Salad Bowls, 158
Chicken
    BBQ Chicken Quinoa Bowls, 86
    Chicken Kofta Bowls, 92
    Chimichurri Chicken Bowls, 87
    Dukkah-Crusted Chicken and Barley
        Bowls, 82
    Ginger Peanut Soba Noodle Bowls, 78
    Green Curry Chicken and Quinoa
        Bowls, 79
    Harissa Chicken Bowls, 83
    Herbed Chicken and Root Vegetable
        Bowls, 93
    Peachy Basil Chicken and Rice Bowls, 88
    Quick Chicken and Sweet Potato Pho
        Bowls, 90
    Quinoa and Chicken Taco Bowls with
        Cilantro-Lime Dressing, 80
    Spicy Thai Chicken and Brown Rice
        Bowls, 89
    Warm Autumn Chicken and Wild Rice
        Bowls, 85
Chickpeas, canned
    Beet Falafel Bowls, 150
    Cauliflower Falafel Power Bowls, 124
    Greek Power Bowls, 107
    Harissa Chicken Bowls, 83
    Herbed Chickpea and Bulgur Bowls, 125
    Masala Chickpea Bowls, 140
    Moroccan-Spiced Chickpea Bowls, 146
    Scrambled Chickpea Breakfast Bowls, 49
    Za'atar Chickpea Bowls, 120
Chili-Maple Tofu Bowls, 139
Chili-Lime Portobello Bowls, 154
Chimichurri Chicken Bowls, 87
Chimichurri Sauce, 19

Chipotle Sweet Potato Bowls, 145
Chocolate-Tahini Chia Pudding Bowls, 168
Chorizo, Mexican
    Black Bean and Chorizo Bowls, 46
Coconut Chia and Tropical Fruit Bowls, 169
Cod fillets
    Tomato-Braised Cod and Barley Bowls, 65
Corn
    Chili-Lime Portobello Bowls, 154
    Chipotle Sweet Potato Bowls, 145
    Lentil and Roasted Tomatillo Bowls, 127
    Summertime Green Goddess Steak
        Bowls, 99
    Sweet Potato and Lentil Taco Bowls, 144
Creamy Feta Sauce, 20
Creamy Freekeh Bowls with Honey-Balsamic
    Stewed Strawberries, 162
Crispy Potato and Smoked Salmon Power
    Bowls, 51
Crispy White Bean and Pesto Bowls, 117
Cucumbers
    Beet Falafel Bowls, 150
    Cauliflower Tabbouleh Bowls with Lamb
        Meatballs, 112
    Crispy Potato and Smoked Salmon Power
        Bowls, 51
    Moroccan Salmon and Millet Bowls, 61
    Peachy Basil Chicken and Rice Bowls, 88
    Raita, 25
    Shrimp Summer Roll Bowls, 69
    Smoked Salmon and Soba Noodle
        Bowls, 58
    Vegetarian Sushi Bowls, 132
    Vietnamese Zucchini Noodle and Shrimp
        Bowls, 70

**D**

Dates, pitted
    Chocolate-Tahini Chia Pudding Bowls, 168
    Dukkah-Crusted Chicken and Barley Bowls, 82

**E**

Edamame
    Brown Rice Bowls with Seared Fish and
        Chimichurri, 75
    Chili-Maple Tofu Bowls, 139
    Salmon Teriyaki Bowls with Miso-Braised
        Kale, 64
    Sesame Tuna Bowls, 66
    Smoked Salmon and Soba Noodle
        Bowls, 58
    Super Green Quinoa Bowls, 116

Eggplants
  Stuffed Eggplant Bowls with Spiced Lamb, 108
Eggs
  Black Bean and Chorizo Bowls, 46
  Broccoli Rice and Egg Bowls, 134
  Brown Rice and Kale Pesto Bowls, 122
  Buckwheat and Black Bean Breakfast Bowls, 48
  Cauliflower Pad Thai Bowls, 135
  Crispy Potato and Smoked Salmon Power Bowls, 51
  Lentil and Smoked Salmon Niçoise Bowls, 56
  Moroccan-Spiced Chickpea Bowls, 146
  Slow Cooker Congee Breakfast Bowls, 47
  Slow Cooker Miso Oat and Egg Bowls, 40
  Spinach and Mushroom Pesto Breakfast Bowls, 44
  Spring Soba Bowls, 133
  Turmeric-Roasted Vegetable Bowls, 153
Essential Pesto Sauce with Any Herb or Leafy Greens, 21
Ethiopian-Spiced Red Lentil Bowls with Greens, 152

F
Fennel bulbs
  Bittersweet Citrus and Salmon Power Bowls, 62
  Dukkah-Crusted Chicken and Barley Bowls, 82
  Harissa Chicken Bowls, 83
  Lentil and Smoked Salmon Niçoise Bowls, 56
  Peachy Basil Chicken and Rice Bowls, 88
Feta cheese
  Buckwheat and Black Bean Breakfast Bowls, 48
  Creamy Feta Sauce, 20
Fish fillets, white
  Brown Rice Bowls with Seared Fish and Chimichurri, 75
  Freekeh Bowls with Caramelized Onions, Warm Tomatoes, and Seared Fish, 73

G
Ginger Beef Bowls, 105
Ginger Peanut Soba Noodle Bowls, 78
Gluten-free recipes
  Almond-Quinoa and Salmon Bowls, 57
  BBQ Chicken Quinoa Bowls, 86
  Black Bean and Chorizo Bowls, 46
  Blackberry Millet Breakfast Bowls, 32

Broccoli Rice and Egg Bowls, 134
Brown Rice and Kale Pesto Bowls, 122
Brown Rice Bowls with Seared Fish and Chimichurri, 75
Buckwheat and Black Bean Breakfast Bowls, 48
Chamomile Poached Pear Bowls, 167
Chili-Lime Portobello Bowls, 154
Chimichurri Chicken Bowls, 87
Chipotle Sweet Potato Bowls, 145
Chocolate-Tahini Chia Pudding Bowls, 168
Coconut Chia and Tropical Fruit Bowls, 169
Coconut Quinoa Breakfast Bowls, 30
Crispy Potato and Smoked Salmon Power Bowls, 51
Ethiopian-Spiced Red Lentil Bowls with Greens, 152
Ginger Peanut Soba Noodle Bowls, 78
Golden Milk Chia Seed Breakfast Bowls, 42
grain alternatives, 12
Green Curry Chicken and Quinoa Bowls, 79
Green Goddess Quinoa Bowls with Crispy Tofu, 119
Harvest Macro Bowl, 142
Herbed Chicken and Root Vegetable Bowls, 93
Korean-Style Beef Bowls with Zucchini Noodles, 102
Lamb Kebab Bowls, 109
Lentil and Roasted Tomatillo Bowls, 127
Lentil and Smoked Salmon Niçoise Bowls, 56
Lime-Avocado Pudding Bowls, 166
Maple-Masala Winter Squash Breakfast Bowls, 37
Maple-Vanilla Overnight Oat Bowls, 34
Masala Chickpea Bowls, 140
Moroccan Salmon and Millet Bowls, 61
Quick Chicken and Sweet Potato Pho Bowls, 90
Quinoa and Chicken Taco Bowls with Cilantro-Lime Dressing, 80
Scrambled Chickpea Breakfast Bowls, 49
Slow Cooker Congee Breakfast Bowls, 47
Smoked Salmon and Soba Noodle Bowls, 58
Smoky Lemon Brussels Sprout Bowls with Turkey Meatballs, 94
Spiced Bean and Mushroom Bowls with Roasted Red Pepper Sauce, 141
Spicy Thai Chicken and Brown Rice Bowls, 89

Spinach and Mushroom Pesto Breakfast Bowls, 44
Spring Soba Bowls, 133
Steak Fajita Spaghetti Squash Bowls, 98
Summertime Green Goddess Steak Bowls, 99
Superfood Salmon Bowls, 74
Sweet Potato and Lentil Taco Bowls, 144
Sweet Potato Breakfast Bowls, 39
Thai Coconut Curry Bowls, 131
Tofu Scramble Bowls with Kale and Brussels Sprouts, 52
Turkey and Cabbage Stir-Fry Bowls with Almond Butter Sauce, 95
Turmeric-Ginger Cauliflower and Lentil Bowls, 143
Turmeric-Roasted Vegetable Bowls, 153
Vietnamese Zucchini Noodle and Shrimp Bowls, 70
Vitamin C Papaya Bowls, 43
Warm Autumn Chicken and Wild Rice Bowls, 85
Winter Chili Bowls with Beef, Beans, and Greens, 106
Za'atar Chickpea Bowls, 120
Goat cheese
  Light and Creamy Goat Cheese Sauce, 22
Golden Milk Chia Seed Breakfast Bowls, 42
Grapefruit, pink
  Dukkah-Crusted Chicken and Barley Bowls, 82
  Vitamin C Papaya Bowls, 43
  Winter Fruit Salad Bowls, 161
Greek Power Bowls, 107
Green beans
  Lentil and Smoked Salmon Niçoise Bowls, 56
  Thai Coconut Curry Bowls, 131
Green Curry Chicken and Quinoa Bowls, 79
Green Goddess Quinoa Bowls with Crispy Tofu, 119

H
Harissa Chicken Bowls, 83
Harvest Macro Bowl, 142
Herbed Chicken and Root Vegetable Bowls, 93
Herbed Chickpea and Bulgur Bowls, 125

J
Jalapeños
  Chili-Lime Portobello Bowls, 154

**K**

Kale
  Beet Falafel Bowls, 150
  Brown Rice and Kale Pesto Bowls, 122
  Buckwheat and Black Bean Breakfast
    Bowls, 48
  Butternut Squash and Kale Bowls, 126
  Crispy White Bean and Pesto Bowls, 117
  Miso Noodle Bowls with Stir-Fried
    Beef, 103
  Moroccan-Spiced Chickpea Bowls, 146
  Salmon Teriyaki Bowls with Miso-Braised
    Kale, 64
  Super Green Quinoa Bowls, 116
  Superfood Salmon Bowls, 74
  Tofu Scramble Bowls with Kale and
    Brussels Sprouts, 52
  Turmeric-Ginger Cauliflower and Lentil
    Bowls, 143
  Turmeric-Roasted Vegetable Bowls, 153
  Winter Chili Bowls with Beef, Beans, and
    Greens, 106
  Za'atar Chickpea Bowls, 120
Kiwis
  Vitamin C Papaya Bowls, 43
Korean-Style Beef Bowls with Zucchini
  Noodles, 102

**L**

Lamb
  Cauliflower Tabbouleh Bowls with Lamb
    Meatballs, 112
  Greek Power Bowls, 107
  Lamb and Roasted Cauliflower Taco Bowls
    with Chimichurri, 113
  Lamb Kebab Bowls, 109
  Lamb Meatball Bowls with Sweet Potato
    Noodles and Green Tahini, 110
  Lentil Quinoa Bowls with Harissa Lamb
    Meatballs, 111
  Stuffed Eggplant Bowls with Spiced
    Lamb, 108
Lentil and Roasted Tomatillo Bowls, 127
Lentil and Smoked Salmon Niçoise Bowls, 56
Lentil Quinoa Bowls with Harissa Lamb
  Meatballs, 111
Light and Creamy Goat Cheese Sauce, 22

**M**

Mangoes
  Coconut Chia and Tropical Fruit Bowls, 169
  Sesame Tuna Bowls, 66
Maple-Masala Winter Squash Breakfast
  Bowls, 37

Maple-Vanilla Overnight Oat Bowls, 34
Masala Chickpea Bowls, 140
Milk
  Apple Pie Farro Breakfast Bowls, 31
  Blackberry Millet Breakfast Bowls, 32
  Chai-Spiced Multigrain Porridge Bowls, 38
  Chamomile Poached Pear Bowls, 167
  Creamy Freekeh Bowls with Honey-
    Balsamic Stewed Strawberries, 162
  Lamb Meatball Bowls with Sweet Potato
    Noodles and Green Tahini, 110
  Maple-Vanilla Overnight Oat Bowls, 34
Milk, coconut
  Coconut Chia and Tropical Fruit Bowls, 169
  Coconut Quinoa Breakfast Bowls, 30
  Ethiopian-Spiced Red Lentil Bowls with
    Greens, 152
  Green Curry Chicken and Quinoa
    Bowls, 79
  Thai Coconut Curry Bowls, 131
Milk, nut
  Chocolate-Tahini Chia Pudding Bowls, 168
  Coconut Chia and Tropical Fruit Bowls, 169
  Golden Milk Chia Seed Breakfast Bowls, 42
  Strawberry Banana Nice Cream Bowls, 159
Miso
  Essential Pesto Sauce with Any Herb or
    Leafy Greens, 21
  Miso-Ginger Sauce, 23
  Salmon Teriyaki Bowls with Miso-Braised
    Kale, 64
  Slow Cooker Miso Oat and Egg Bowls, 40
Miso Noodle Bowls with Stir-Fried Beef, 103
Moroccan Salmon and Millet Bowls, 61
Moroccan-Spiced Chickpea Bowls, 146
Mung beans
  Winter Squash and Farro Macro
    Bowls, 149
Mushrooms
  Balsamic Shrimp and Farro Bowls, 72
  Chili-Lime Portobello Bowls, 154
  Ginger Beef Bowls, 105
  Ginger Peanut Soba Noodle Bowls, 78
  Quick Chicken and Sweet Potato Pho
    Bowls, 90
  Slow Cooker Congee Breakfast Bowls, 47
  Smoky Lemon Brussels Sprout Bowls with
    Turkey Meatballs, 94
  Spiced Bean and Mushroom Bowls with
    Roasted Red Pepper Sauce, 141
  Spinach and Mushroom Pesto Breakfast
    Bowls, 44
  Spring Soba Bowls, 133

**O**

Oils, healthy, 9
Olives, kalamata
  Greek Power Bowls, 107
Orange blossom water
  Chamomile Poached Pear Bowls, 167
  Pomegranate and Freekeh Breakfast
    Tabbouleh Bowls, 35
Oranges
  Bittersweet Citrus and Salmon Power
    Bowls, 62
  Vitamin C Papaya Bowls, 43
  Winter Fruit Salad Bowls, 161

**P**

Papayas
  Vitamin C Papaya Bowls, 43
Parsnips
  Herbed Chicken and Root Vegetable
    Bowls, 93
Passion fruit
  Coconut Chia and Tropical Fruit Bowls, 169
Peaches
  Peachy Basil Chicken and Rice Bowls, 88
  Summer Fruit Salad Bowls, 158
Peanut butter
  Ginger Peanut Soba Noodle Bowls, 78
  Peanut Sauce, 24
Pears
  Chamomile Poached Pear Bowls, 167
  Winter Fruit Salad Bowls, 161
Persimmons
  Winter Fruit Salad Bowls, 161
Pesto Sauce with Any Herb or Leafy Greens, 21
Pineapple
  Coconut Chia and Tropical Fruit Bowls, 169
Piquillo peppers
  Chimichurri Chicken Bowls, 87
Pistachios
  Brown Rice and Kale Pesto Bowls, 122
Plums
  Ricotta and Honey Roasted Plum Bowls
    with Crunchy Buckwheat, 165
Poblano peppers
  Lentil and Roasted Tomatillo Bowls, 127
Pomegranate arils
  Pomegranate and Freekeh Breakfast
    Tabbouleh Bowls, 35
  Winter Fruit Salad Bowls, 161
Potatoes, fingerling
  Crispy Potato and Smoked Salmon Power
    Bowls, 51
  Lentil and Smoked Salmon Niçoise
    Bowls, 56

Protein sources, 9
Pumpkin Pie Cheesecake Bowls, 160

**Q**
Quick Chicken and Sweet Potato Pho
    Bowls, 90
Quinoa and Chicken Taco Bowls with
    Cilantro-Lime Dressing, 80

**R**
Radicchio
    Beef and Broccoli Bowls, 100
    Bittersweet Citrus and Salmon Power
        Bowls, 62
    Butternut Squash and Kale Bowls, 126
    Freekeh Bowls with Caramelized Onions,
        Warm Tomatoes, and Seared Fish, 73
Radishes
    Banh Mi Bowls, 128
    Broccoli Rice and Egg Bowls, 134
    Buckwheat and Black Bean Breakfast
        Bowls, 48
    Crispy White Bean and Pesto Bowls, 117
    Ginger Beef Bowls, 105
    Lamb and Roasted Cauliflower Taco Bowls
        with Chimichurri, 113
    Lentil and Roasted Tomatillo Bowls, 127
    Quick Chicken and Sweet Potato Pho
        Bowls, 90
    Shrimp Summer Roll Bowls, 69
    Slow Cooker Miso Oat and Egg Bowls, 40
    Spring Soba Bowls, 133
    Turmeric-Roasted Vegetable Bowls, 153
    Winter Chili Bowls with Beef, Beans, and
        Greens, 106
Raita, 25
Red peppers, jarred roasted
    Roasted Red Pepper Sauce, 25
Ricotta and Honey Roasted Plum Bowls with
    Crunchy Buckwheat, 165
Romaine
    Banh Mi Bowls, 128
    Harvest Macro Bowl, 142
    Shrimp Summer Roll Bowls, 69
Rose water
    Summer Fruit Salad Bowls, 158

**S**
Salmon
    Almond-Quinoa and Salmon Bowls, 57
    Bittersweet Citrus and Salmon Power
        Bowls, 62
    Crispy Potato and Smoked Salmon Power
        Bowls, 51

Lentil and Smoked Salmon Niçoise
    Bowls, 56
Moroccan Salmon and Millet Bowls, 61
Salmon Teriyaki Bowls with Miso-Braised
    Kale, 64
Superfood Salmon Bowls, 74
Scrambled Chickpea Breakfast Bowls, 49
Serrano Chilis
    Masala Chickpea Bowls, 140
Sesame Tuna Bowls, 66
Shrimp
    Balsamic Shrimp and Farro Bowls, 72
    Shrimp Summer Roll Bowls, 69
    Vietnamese Zucchini Noodle and Shrimp
        Bowls, 70
Slow Cooker Congee Breakfast Bowls, 47
Slow Cooker Miso Oat and Egg Bowls, 40
Smoked Salmon and Soba Noodle Bowls, 58
Smoky Lemon Brussels Sprout Bowls with
    Turkey Meatballs, 94
Snap peas
    Green Goddess Quinoa Bowls with Crispy
        Tofu, 119
    Quick Chicken and Sweet Potato Pho
        Bowls, 90
Snow peas
    Ginger Beef Bowls, 105
Soyrizo
    Black Bean and Chorizo Bowls, 46
Spiced Bean and Mushroom Bowls with
    Roasted Red Pepper Sauce, 141
Spicy Sesame Tofu and Rice Bowls, 136
Spicy Thai Chicken and Brown Rice Bowls, 89
Spinach, baby
    BBQ Chicken Quinoa Bowls, 86
    Black Bean and Chorizo Bowls, 46
    Broccoli Rice and Egg Bowls, 134
    Chipotle Sweet Potato Bowls, 145
    Crispy Potato and Smoked Salmon Power
        Bowls, 51
    Ethiopian-Spiced Red Lentil Bowls with
        Greens, 152
    Korean-Style Beef Bowls with Zucchini
        Noodles, 102
    Peachy Basil Chicken and Rice Bowls, 88
    Scrambled Chickpea Breakfast Bowls, 49
    Slow Cooker Congee Breakfast Bowls, 47
    Spinach and Mushroom Pesto Breakfast
        Bowls, 44
    Stuffed Eggplant Bowls with Spiced
        Lamb, 108
    Tomato-Braised Cod and Barley Bowls, 65
Spring Soba Bowls, 133

Squash
    Butternut Squash and Kale Bowls, 126
    Harvest Macro Bowl, 142
    Maple-Masala Winter Squash Breakfast
        Bowls, 37
    Steak Fajita Spaghetti Squash Bowls, 98
    Summertime Green Goddess Steak
        Bowls, 99
    Warm Autumn Chicken and Wild Rice
        Bowls, 85
    Winter Squash and Farro Macro
        Bowls, 149
Star fruit
    Coconut Chia and Tropical Fruit Bowls, 169
Steak Fajita Spaghetti Squash Bowls, 98
Strawberries
    Creamy Freekeh Bowls with Honey-
        Balsamic Stewed Strawberries, 162
    Strawberry Banana Nice Cream Bowls, 159
    Summer Fruit Salad Bowls, 158
Stuffed Eggplant Bowls with Spiced
    Lamb, 108
Summer Fruit Salad Bowls, 158
Summertime Green Goddess Steak Bowls, 99
Super Green Quinoa Bowls, 116
Sweet potatoes
    BBQ Chicken Quinoa Bowls, 86
    Chipotle Sweet Potato Bowls, 145
    Green Curry Chicken and Quinoa
        Bowls, 79
    Herbed Chicken and Root Vegetable
        Bowls, 93
    Quick Chicken and Sweet Potato Pho
        Bowls, 90
    Superfood Salmon Bowls, 74
    Sweet Potato and Lentil Taco Bowls, 144
    Sweet Potato Breakfast Bowls, 39
    Tofu Scramble Bowls with Kale and
        Brussels Sprouts, 52
    Turmeric-Ginger Cauliflower and Lentil
        Bowls, 143

**T**
Tahini Sauce, 26
Thai Coconut Curry Bowls, 131
Tofu, extra-firm
    Banh Mi Bowls, 128
    Cauliflower Pad Thai Bowls, 135
    Chili-Maple Tofu Bowls, 139
    Green Goddess Quinoa Bowls with Crispy
        Tofu, 119
    Spicy Sesame Tofu and Rice Bowls, 136
    Thai Coconut Curry Bowls, 131

Tofu Scramble Bowls with Kale and
Brussels Sprouts, 52
Vegetarian Sushi Bowls, 132
Tomatillos
Lentil and Roasted Tomatillo Bowls, 127
Tomatoes, canned
Masala Chickpea Bowls, 140
Moroccan-Spiced Chickpea Bowls, 146
Tomato-Braised Cod and Barley Bowls, 65
Winter Chili Bowls with Beef, Beans, and
Greens, 106
Tomatoes, fresh
Cauliflower Tabbouleh Bowls with Lamb
Meatballs, 112
Chili-Lime Portobello Bowls, 154
Freekeh Bowls with Caramelized Onions,
Warm Tomatoes, and Seared Fish, 73
Greek Power Bowls, 107
Harissa Chicken Bowls, 83
Lamb Kebab Bowls, 109
Lentil and Smoked Salmon Niçoise
Bowls, 56
Quinoa and Chicken Taco Bowls with
Cilantro-Lime Dressing, 80
Steak Fajita Spaghetti Squash Bowls, 98
Turkey, ground
Smoky Lemon Brussels Sprout Bowls with
Turkey Meatballs, 94
Turkey and Cabbage Stir-Fry Bowls with
Almond Butter Sauce, 95
Turmeric-Ginger Cauliflower and Lentil
Bowls, 143
Turmeric-Roasted Vegetable Bowls, 153

V
Vegan recipes
Butternut Squash and Kale Bowls, 126
Cauliflower Falafel Power Bowls, 124
Chili-Maple Tofu Bowls, 139
Chili-Lime Portobello Bowls, 154
Chipotle Sweet Potato Bowls, 145
Chocolate-Tahini Chia Pudding Bowls, 168
Coconut Chia and Tropical Fruit Bowls, 169
Golden Milk Chia Seed Breakfast Bowls, 42
Harvest Macro Bowl, 142
Herbed Chickpea and Bulgur Bowls, 125
Lentil and Roasted Tomatillo Bowls, 127
Scrambled Chickpea Breakfast Bowls, 49
Spiced Bean and Mushroom Bowls with
Roasted Red Pepper Sauce, 141
Strawberry Banana Nice Cream Bowls, 159
Summer Fruit Salad Bowls, 158
Sweet Potato Breakfast Bowls, 39
Thai Coconut Curry Bowls, 131

Tofu Scramble Bowls with Kale and
Brussels Sprouts, 52
Vitamin C Papaya Bowls, 43
Winter Fruit Salad Bowls, 161
Vegetarian recipes
Apple Pie Farro Breakfast Bowls, 31
Banh Mi Bowls, 128
Beet Falafel Bowls, 150
Blackberry Millet Breakfast Bowls, 32
Broccoli Rice and Egg Bowls, 134
Brown Rice and Kale Pesto Bowls, 122
Buckwheat and Black Bean Breakfast
Bowls, 48
Chai-Spiced Multigrain Porridge Bowls, 38
Chamomile Poached Pear Bowls, 167
Coconut Quinoa Breakfast Bowls, 30
Creamy Freekeh Bowls with Honey-
Balsamic Stewed Strawberries, 162
Crispy White Bean and Pesto Bowls, 117
Ethiopian-Spiced Red Lentil Bowls with
Greens, 152
Green Goddess Quinoa Bowls with Crispy
Tofu, 119
Lime-Avocado Pudding Bowls, 166
Maple-Masala Winter Squash Breakfast
Bowls, 37
Maple-Vanilla Overnight Oat Bowls, 34
Masala Chickpea Bowls, 140
Moroccan-Spiced Chickpea Bowls, 146
Pomegranate and Freekeh Breakfast
Tabbouleh Bowls, 35
Pumpkin Pie Cheesecake Bowls, 160
Ricotta and Honey Roasted Plum Bowls
with Crunchy Buckwheat, 165
Slow Cooker Congee Breakfast Bowls, 47
Slow Cooker Miso Oat and Egg Bowls, 40
Spicy Sesame Tofu and Rice Bowls, 136
Spinach and Mushroom Pesto Breakfast
Bowls, 44
Spring Soba Bowls, 133
Sweet Potato and Lentil Taco Bowls, 144
Turmeric-Ginger Cauliflower and Lentil
Bowls, 143
Turmeric-Roasted Vegetable Bowls, 153
Vegetarian Sushi Bowls, 132
Winter Squash and Farro Macro
Bowls, 149
Za'atar Chickpea Bowls, 120
Vietnamese Zucchini Noodle and Shrimp
Bowls, 70
Vitamin C Papaya Bowls, 43

W
Walnuts
Superfood Salmon Bowls, 74
Warm Autumn Chicken and Wild Rice
Bowls, 85
Watercress
Brown Rice Bowls with Seared Fish and
Chimichurri, 75
Lamb Kebab Bowls, 109
Winter Chili Bowls with Beef, Beans, and
Greens, 106
Winter Fruit Salad Bowls, 161
Winter Squash and Farro Macro Bowls, 149

Y
Yogurt
Avocado Green Goddess Dressing, 16
Blackberry Millet Breakfast Bowls, 32
Chamomile Poached Pear Bowls, 167
Coconut Chia and Tropical Fruit Bowls, 169
Creamy Freekeh Bowls with Honey-
Balsamic Stewed Strawberries, 162
Lime-Avocado Pudding Bowls, 166
Maple-Masala Winter Squash Breakfast
Bowls, 37
Maple-Vanilla Overnight Oat Bowls, 34
Pomegranate and Freekeh Breakfast
Tabbouleh Bowls, 35
Pumpkin Pie Cheesecake Bowls, 160
Raita, 25
Vitamin C Papaya Bowls, 43
Yogurt Sauce, 27

Z
Za'atar Chickpea Bowls, 120
Zucchini
Balsamic Shrimp and Farro Bowls, 72
Harissa Chicken Bowls, 83
Korean-Style Beef Bowls with Zucchini
Noodles, 102
Lamb Kebab Bowls, 109
Spinach and Mushroom Pesto Breakfast
Bowls, 44
Summertime Green Goddess Steak
Bowls, 99
Super Green Quinoa Bowls, 116
Thai Coconut Curry Bowls, 131
Turkey and Cabbage Stir-Fry Bowls with
Almond Butter Sauce, 95
Vietnamese Zucchini Noodle and Shrimp
Bowls, 70